THE ARCHITECT
AND THE COMPUTER

BOYD AUGER

THE ARCHITECT AND THE COMPUTER

PALL MALL

Pall Mall Press
5 Cromwell Place, London SW7

First published in Great Britain 1972
© 1972 by Pall Mall Press, London
ISBN 0 269 02798 X

Printed in Great Britain by
Butler & Tanner Ltd, Frome and London

CONTENTS

INTRODUCTION

My object in writing this book has been to stimulate a wider interest in the application of computers to building design, and by outlining what I see as the historical relevance of these applications, present the electronic computer in perspective with the problems now facing the architectural profession.

Until quite recently, the work on computer aids for architects appeared fragmented and largely unrelated to normal office practice, and it has been very difficult to give reasons for the confidence many of us have felt that these machines would prove to have great significance for the profession.

Now, however, a pattern is beginning to emerge, and although it is still far from complete, it is possible to see the computer in the context of the architect's office, both in terms of working method and financial capacity.

The introduction of the so-called mini-computer to information handling is probably the most significant development in computers for some years, as it provides a low-cost computing capacity which closely matches the requirements of the small office. For this reason, a large part of the book is devoted to describing a system which uses one of these machines to aid in the preparation of construction information.

Many architectural design problems, however, when programmed for solution by a computer, require to be processed on much larger machines. The office terminal linked to a multi-access computer appears the most logical way to do this, and the use of a terminal as an extension to an office system is also considered.

The application of computers to these large design problems is still at an early stage, and many methods are being considered and developed. It would appear, however, that three techniques have particular promise and these have been described in some detail in Chapter 6.

Also included is a general description of the operation of a typical medium-size computer, and the use of flowcharts for programming.

Emphasis has been placed throughout upon flowcharts, as I feel that the best way for a practising architect, like myself, to prepare a computer program is by the preparation of flowcharts. The actual programming is best left to an expert.

Finally, I would like to state what this book is not. It is not a catalogue of programs, nor is it an attempt to describe all the work in progress in this field. I have limited myself to building design and generally have described techniques rather than programs.

The application of computers to large-scale planning problems is outside my theme, and I have not mentioned project management aids, like critical path analysis, because they have been detailed many times elsewhere. The programs I have described have been chosen because I know them well.

I have tried to give credit, mostly in the references, to those who have provided me directly with information for this book, but if everybody to whom I am indebted for knowledge about computer applications was included, the list would be as long as the book. I wish especially to acknowledge the immense help I have received from my colleagues in the Departments of Engineering at Leicester University and the Imperial College of Science and Technology, London. In particular to Dr. Geoffrey Butlin and Mr. Alan Jebb who have each read large sections of the manuscript and provided valuable comments. I am also very much indebted to Miss Joanna Goodchild who converted nine or ten hours of my tape recordings into a readable typescript, and to Mr. Jean-Claude Peissel and Mrs. Anne Engel of the Pall Mall Press.

To Dr. Pangloss

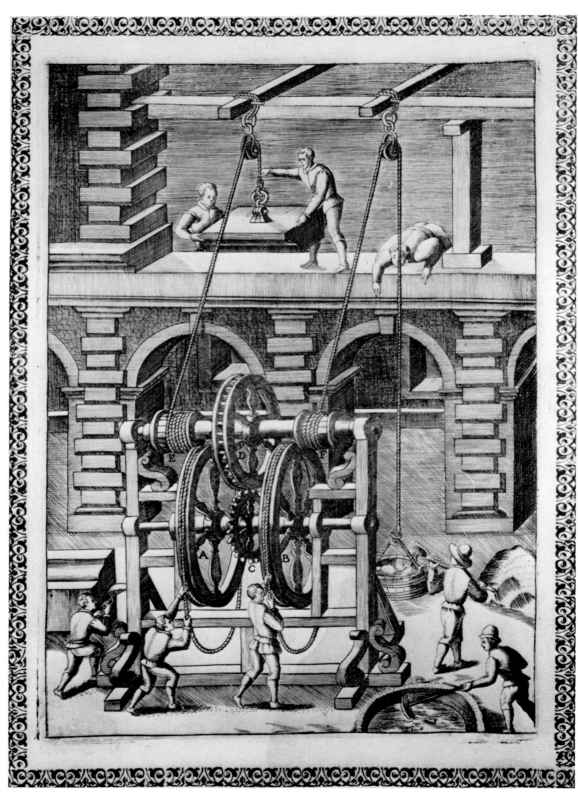

1 THE ARCHITECT

1.1 The Client

When a client commissions an architect he expects and he usually gets a design which fits his site and serves his needs. He also gets a work of art. Unless he is naïve he will expect this, for it has been accepted by every civilization in recorded history that any edifice large enough to compete to some degree with nature should be a thing of beauty, and beauty to be relevant must have originality, which in this context is called art. If the origins of this acceptance lay in a need to achieve order or placate the Gods, the architect–client relationship would be simple and rational. In practice, however, the force behind this apparently unifying and universally accepted principle is often a very disuniting desire for self-expression on the part of both the architect and his client.

The innate desire for self-expression is in all men and each achieves his own outlet in his work or private life, but when faced with the need to build, few cannot but respond to the monumental potential of the medium, no matter how far removed it is from his normal creative outlets.

Big corporations and government departments, although apparently anonymous in their actions, in fact reflect to a considerable extent the creative interests of their executives. Thus when they build, individuals will be drawn to exert their influence and confuse, like other clients, their practical needs with their personal aspirations.

To the architect this can be a serious problem, but it is also his *raison d'être*. The architect exists to provide the skill necessary to achieve what the client has initially conceived. That the client is the prime mover in this respect gives him an edge on the situation, and he often only comes to accept the need for an architect when faced with his own lack of time or expertise. He will, in fact, only become fully resigned to the situation when the architect's skill becomes so evident that he is convinced that the design will be of a totally different quality to that which he conceived.

When this happens, the architect–client relationship is at its most creative, drawing the maximum power from both sides towards the production of a building which is the architect's expression of his client's aspirations through the medium of the culture they share.

It is strange that in spite of the fact that this relationship between client and architect is of prime importance and should clearly be the first to be considered when changes in the profession are contemplated, it is in practice rarely discussed except at the level of historical gossip.

It would appear inevitable that the computer techniques described and foreseen in this book will bring about a major reshaping of architectural practice. It therefore seems logical to start with a brief consideration of the architect–client relationship so that the potential of the computer can be seen in these terms.

1.2 The Master Mason and 'L'Uomo Universale'

We know very little about the architects of Classical Greece and Rome, which is hardly surprising as we know very little about anyone of this period apart from the ruling classes and a handful of writers. Only in the last thousand years have the daily affairs of men been recorded on a scale that will allow us to assess the origins of our present professional situation. This round figure of a thousand years coincides in Western Europe with a great expansion of learning, art and building, which from the start has been founded on individual skill and prestige.

The medieval mason is the first architect about whom we know more than just a name. His status initially was that of a craftsman, and it is clear that what changed this hired hand into a valued consultant over a period of two hundred years was expertise. At least in cathedral building, his prestige rose coincidently with the height of the vaults that he built. Over the period of the twelfth and thirteenth centuries, the master mason changed from an anonymous craftsman to a named and sought-after expert, and by the end of the fourteenth century his occupation had become one in which a gentleman could dabble.

As late as 1130 the Abbé Suger took all the credit for the rebuilding of Saint-Denis, in spite of the fact that his master mason was of undoubted genius. By 1288, however, the centre stone of the nave of Amiens Cathedral was inscribed for the consecration with the names of the King, the Bishop and the three 'Masters of Works' who had built it over a period of sixty-eight years. In Notre Dame de Paris, the name of the mason, Master Jehan de Chelles, was inscribed on the wall of the south transept. The inscription is twenty-five feet long.

This increased status probably evolved not only from the value of the mason's specialist knowledge, but also from the general learning which he acquired when travelling and studying. When a major building was under construction, a rare event in most districts, the mason's site hut or lodge became a centre for the local intelligentsia who met to discuss with the masons the theory behind their building skills.

Much has been made of the secretiveness of the medieval masons regarding their craft. Since, however, it was their skill which really mattered, one can assume that the various parlour games they devised, like how to draw a square which is twice the area of another square, were intended to entertain their visitors and provide a personal involvement between themselves and potential future clients.

In Scotland, lack of suitable stone for carving by which the mason could be distinguished from the cowan (dry stone wall

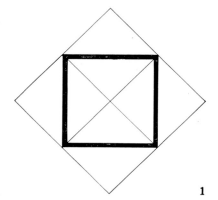

1

12

builder) drove the masons to use secret signs which it appears they acquired from witchcraft.

In England and France, however, the social relationship between architect and client which started in these medieval lodges needed only the humanism of the Renaissance to raise the design of buildings to the level of an intellectual occupation, and the architect to his present status.

The fourteenth century with its Hundred Years War and Black Death saw a massive decline in craftsmanship but also a similarly large expansion of scholarship, thus setting the scene for the Renaissance and the intellectualization of architecture. This intellectualization did not result initially in any significant change in the origins of the architects. Most were craftsmen who were trained in the powerful European guilds, and it was not until Leon Battista Alberti that we find an architect who is of patrician origin and without a craft training.

Alberti came to architecture through the study of Roman ruins, and in 1450 published the first Renaissance books of architecture. His relatively high social status gave him the education necessary to write on all that interested him and to understand all that was understood in his day. Thus he set a standard which led to the concept of the architect as the universal man, *L'Uomo Universale*, to which most architects have aspired ever since.

In the process he also formulated, unintentionally one must assume, a new architect–client relationship. The consultant craftsman who with the Renaissance had become the consultant–artist was now the universal consultant. A man who, although socially inferior to his aristocratic clients, was intellectually their equal and able to provide an answer to most problems in building and the related arts and sciences. This ideal relationship became the norm for nearly four hundred years and helped to lift architecture to a peak of refinement in later centuries.

1.3 The Modern Movement

The majority of clients in any period of history come from the class which is in control of the major part of the nation's wealth. The classes who have held this enviable position in Europe have changed regularly every two hundred years. In the thirteenth century it was the Church, by the fifteenth century Royalty, in the seventeenth century the Nobility and in the nineteenth it became the turn of the middle class, entrepreneurs of commerce and industry. Each change must have brought great problems for the architects involved but none so great as the last. Church, Royalty and Nobility had all provided a small enlightened and largely omnipotent homogeneous group from which the architect could obtain most of the sanctions he required to carry out his work.

The Industrial Revolution in Britain dramatically changed this situation. The wealth of the country was vastly increased, but was spread widely over a class who were numbered in thousands. A class moreover whose education was obtained from a school system designed largely to prepare their social betters for the universities to which they themselves rarely aspired. Thus it is that, at the end of the eighteenth century, one finds the architectural profession turning in upon itself, unable to obtain intellectual stimulus from its *clientèle*, while failing to keep contact with the scientific advances of the age, a full understanding of which was essential to *L'Uomo Universale*.

This break with advanced learning had many causes. As the nineteenth century advanced, the various learned societies declined and the universities, always somewhat unworldly places, became the centres of scientific thought. Professional boundaries started to harden, while the increased scale of building and the introduction of structural steel immensely widened the field of knowledge required in architectural education.

The claustrophobic condition of architectural thought in the latter part of the eighteenth century led inevitably to self-doubt. The necessity for architectural change was evident. For nearly a hundred years the argument went on and was seen almost entirely in terms of a search for a relevant style. Gothic had suited the Middle Ages, Classical had suited the Renaissance—what style would suit the Industrial Revolution? By 1850 it was evident that almost any style from Anglo-Saxon to Chinoiserie had its uses but none appeared fully relevant to the machine age. Then came the Crystal Palace.

The impact of this building on the profession went much deeper than one would now suspect. Today we think of the Crystal Palace in terms of the architectonic pile which stood on Sydenham Hill for eighty years, but the building constructed in Hyde Park in 1851 for the Great Exhibition was a much more simple structure, and the design first published in the *Illustrated London News* on 6 July 1850 and subsequently republished in almost every paper in England was more simple still.[1] This initial design must have been seen by practically every architect in Britain and most in Europe. The original Crystal Palace was the archetypal glass box, and its construction included the use of power-operated site machines, the hydraulic testing on site of cast-iron beams, with extensive prefabrication, and coordinated site assembly by teamwork. All of which resulted in a building with a floor area of a million square feet, which had first been sketched on a blotter in June, being occupied by the client on 31 December of the same year. The designer, Joseph Paxton, was a modest man and disinclined to boast of the originality of his design, but many other engineers were quick to point out that this project's success was

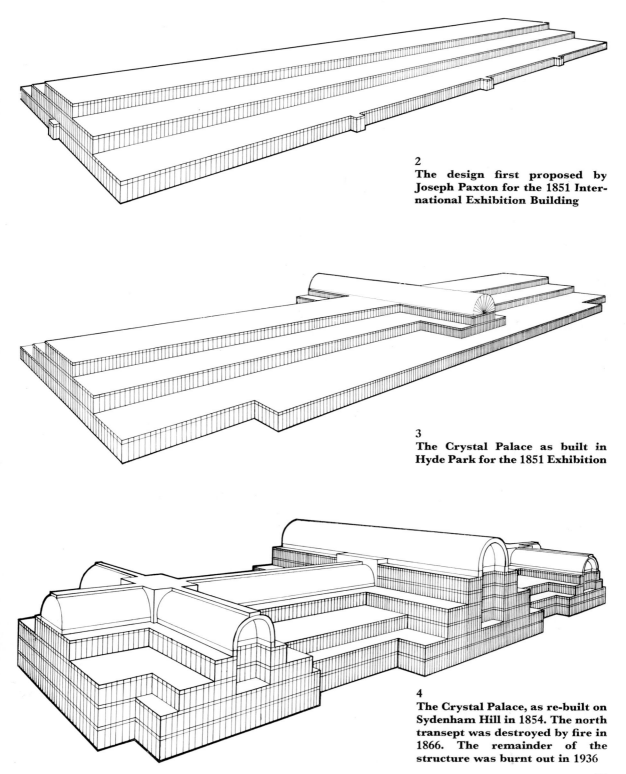

2
The design first proposed by
Joseph Paxton for the 1851 International Exhibition Building

3
The Crystal Palace as built in
Hyde Park for the 1851 Exhibition

4
The Crystal Palace, as re-built on
Sydenham Hill in 1854. The north
transept was destroyed by fire in
1866. The remainder of the
structure was burnt out in 1936

due to its lack of 'Architecture'. Some also predicted a future where most buildings would be designed without reference to architectural theory, but in so doing they underrated the influence of the profession.

The outcome was the Arts and Crafts Movement of which William Morris was the most vocal member. Morris, like others, claimed that the contents of the Exhibition of 1851 drove him to turn his back on industry, but the reaction behind the movement, which carried the majority of architects away from reality from that time on to the First World War, was more probably Paxton's building and all that it implied. In one simple gesture this railway engineer and glasshouse designer had proposed a form of construction which provided a more satisfactory environment and a vastly more simple structure than anything the architectural profession in competition had been able to propose and at half the price of the next cheapest scheme.

The Arts and Crafts Movement and the various aesthetic developments which followed from it supplied the profession with the original styles for which it craved. While this was happening, architects rejected the technology which inevitably came to dominate the building industry, and allowed important aspects of their profession to slip away into the hands of others.

By 1850 the building of bridges had already become the preserve of the Civil Engineer. By 1920 the Structural Engineer, Services Engineer and Quantity Surveyor had all taken their places as necessary sub-consultants on major building projects. If during this period an effective mathematical building planning technique had been evolved with its attendant sub-consultant, the architect would probably have sunk to the level of an exterior decorator. By the end of the nineteenth century the occupational classifications had hardened and the architect was cast as an artist.

Thus, when in the early years of this century architects finally came to embrace technology, they did so not at its origin but at the superficial level of appearances. How to make buildings look like machines became the principal preoccupation, while the failure of new materials to live up to the expectations predicted by the architectural science fiction writers became the chief problem. This whole period, right up to the present day, abounds with problems arising from the failure to understand materials or the implications of changing techniques.

The impact of these events upon the architect–client relationship has been disastrous. The architect's failure to provide a unified design and his acceptance of sub-consultants for major parts of it had not gone unnoticed. The purely symbolic nature of most of the stylistic forms adopted in the name of functionalism was often all too obvious to a client, who nevertheless lacked the historic sense to appreciate the problem and the social conviction to counter the architect's evangelistic fervour.

The rapid expansion of building component manufacture in the early years of this century marked a change-over from the site fabrication of buildings to present-day techniques of assembling mostly factory-made elements. The wide range of often totally unrelated components supplied by many thousands of manufacturers, and the research required to make new materials safe to use and new building types workable, combines to produce an information explosion which has become the major preoccupation of the architect today.

The technological level of building industrialization has been of a very low order. Simple mass production processes have been employed to keep down the labour costs involved in producing door knobs, window frames and precast concrete sections, etc., but, with a few exceptions, the capital expenditure has been relatively small and the impact on design insignificant. This has been in marked contrast to the expectations of a long line of architectural prophets who, since the middle of the last century, have predicted the total industrialization of building and in particular the factory-made house.

1.4 Industrialization

The idea of manufacturing whole buildings in large pieces, especially houses, has been a popular one for many years. Attempts made in Britain in 1945 to convert war-time production lines to housing failed in the main. Interest revived again in the early sixties when the first major projects using so-called building 'systems' were started. The most successful were school systems developed by designers employed by groups of local authorities who used their combined purchasing power to induce manufacturers to develop and produce a special range of factory-made components to be assembled on site.

Soon after the appearance of these school systems, a number of major building contractors in Britain took out licences for Danish and French precast concrete high-rise housing systems which also appeared on the market. With promises of support from various government bodies and local authorities, several contractors spent large sums building factories to produce the concrete components required. By 1964 it seemed as if the housing industry was about to go over almost entirely to 'industrialized' building, a term invented to replace 'prefabrication' as the latter was thought to be synonymous with 'temporary' in the public mind. By 1969, however, industrialization in housing was all but dead. Only in school building did it survive, possibly as the result of the efforts of some senior

local authority architects who had the power to enforce the use of their favourite system.

The facts which explain this apparent contradiction of so many fond dreams are really quite simple. The systems were introduced in a period of exceptional economic growth when skilled labour was very difficult to obtain. Both the private developers and the local authorities were very anxious to invest, and were prepared to pay a premium to anyone who could build quickly with the minimum of site labour. By 1968, however, the boom was over. Unemployment had made labour more readily available and lack of finance had removed the urge to build quickly. The principal advantages of industrialized building were therefore cancelled out, and its failings became all too obvious. The failings are not worth enlarging upon except for one which is of long-term significance.

Industrialized housing systems were never able to compete in price with normal building methods except in the single case of high-rise apartment-blocks consisting of concrete slabs with low-cost finishes. As long as the finishes were cheap and maximum advantage could be drawn from a stationary tower crane, then factory-produced components could compete with traditional techniques. This basic principle of industrialized housing was the reason for its failure. If a major component, i.e. a wall, floor, roof, etc., is produced on site from raw materials delivered by a supplier, the finished article should not cost the building owner or client more than twice the cost of the materials and the labour involved in fabricating and placing the component. That is to say, the overheads on a given item should amount to between eighty and one hundred per cent of the labour and materials cost. If, however, the component is factory-made, the overheads are very much greater. The cost of the factory and its site and of the additional facilities required by factory labour, as well as the more sophisticated plant involved, normally result in a component valued at four to five times the materials and labour costs. The component must then be transported to the site and installed. It is therefore evident that factory expenditure on materials and labour must be reduced to about one-third of that on site if the prefabricated component is to be competitive. The object of the sophisticated factory plant is undoubtedly to achieve such reduction. However, unless totally new materials are introduced, the reduction required is virtually impossible to obtain. Furthermore, when new materials are used, an even greater reduction is required to ensure the acceptability of new and untried products. New materials also frequently require large capital expenditure on plant and development, and unless a major price advantage can be shown, the risk is considerable. As a result large factory-made components can only be successfully employed when speed of building and labour are both at a premium, or where the use of the component is guaranteed by a government agency.

The short-lived success of industrialized housing in the mid-sixties was totally dependent upon the client and his architect accepting almost completely what the systems could provide. The architectural profession was aware of some of the obvious faults of the early industrialized systems, while others not so obvious became apparent in later years. Architects took particular exception to the severe restrictions on design inherent in the early systems, and as a result the concept of the so-called 'open' system was canvassed widely.

The open system was in fact a non-system. It consisted of a wide range of housing components to standard dimensions, all interconnecting so that a designer could assemble a building from parts from many different sources. The great fallacy of such a system was its interconnectability. The only universal or near universal connecting system is the hammer and nail.

6
An attempt at medium-rise system building using components made from traditional materials in the factory

Traditional building techniques in housing depend upon the use of established sequences of assembly, which result in materials either holding themselves together by dead weight, or by hammer and nail techniques. Special clips, expanding joints, interlocking wedges, screw levels and spring cover strips just do not compete and fail so completely to do so that it is difficult to see any system which depends upon them being viable in the foreseeable future.

Although it seems unlikely that these or any similar attempts at total prefabrication will meet with success in the future, there are other developments in this field which appear to have brighter prospects. One interesting possibility is the rather special case of the American trailer industry, which has expanded from the production of traditional car caravans into the field of the 'trailer home'. The trailer home sells because of its low price, the prerequisite of any new apparently sub-standard product. It is usually sub-standard in floor area and sound insulation but well equipped. By exploiting the unique situation of an existing industry with its own standards, in a country which appears to possess unlimited space, it has been possible to provide a habitation at a bargain price.

In theory these prefabricated units would appear to be directly applicable to other forms of housing, but the conditions which make this type of construction viable are finely drawn and any major changes result in the concept ceasing to be of relevance. The modular house is a recent development, being a more substantial version of the trailer home, conceived as a permanent dwelling. Production is expanding, but it still caters for a similar client and similar conditions, while all attempts

7
Modular housing in the U.S.A. Factory-produced housing modules constructed by methods originating more from the trailer industry than from the building industry. Developed by Guerdon Industries Inc., jointly with Reynolds Metals company

to use these prefabricated half-house units for high density developments appear so far to have failed.

The modular house is, however, the most logical and commercially sound approach to the industrialization of mass housing we have yet seen, and when, inevitably, large-scale industrialization of housing is achieved, it will probably be with fully equipped whole-house or half-house units of this type. Climatic and labour differences make such developments more likely in North America than in Britain, and a crucial difference in permissible trucking load widths could severely hamper any such system in Britain.

There is, of course, always the possibility of airlifting finished dwellings from factory to site. To do this it is necessary to have a helicopter with a carrying capacity sufficient to lift a dwelling made of economic materials (say, about 20,000 kg or 45,000 lb), and no machine even approaching this size has so far been available.[2] Now, however, at least three machines of this capacity are being developed, so within the next ten years we should see this classic fantasy of modern architecture attempted on a commercial scale.

1.5 The Information Explosion

It is difficult to establish when the filing and retrieval of information first became a problem for the architect, but it had become a subject of major concern by the mid-fifties. Today, keeping abreast of information on new products and building research forms a significant item in the time of any conscientious architect, and an adequate filing system for an office which designs a broad range of building types can be very expensive to maintain.

It has been estimated that if a library was prepared of the products at present available to the architect, assuming that to describe each product in sufficient detail for design and specification would take on average no more than one side of a single sheet of paper, then the resulting volumes would fill eight hundred feet of shelving and the sheets would need to be replaced for updating purposes at the rate of four hundred pages per day. In practice, of course, the average architect's office files details of only a fraction of this total, but the problem is still considerable. The steadily increasing complexity of buildings, especially from the point of view of planning and services, has proved a major problem for the architect, who has found the need to increase his own output of information in the form of drawings, schedules and specifications in order to provide the details required by his sub-consultants and contractors. The correlating, checking, filing and utilization of all this information has greatly increased the quantity of work required today for a major project such as a hospital or town hall. The basic method of working, however, has changed little. Apart from techniques of drawing reproduction, methods of presenting information have changed only in so far as new materials have forced them to do so.

The major change has been in the office organization required to force these outdated methods of information handling to work under the changed conditions. The traditional architectural practice at the beginning of this century consisted of one or more principals, each of whom was aided directly by a small group of assistants. Each principal had a job or number of jobs depending upon size which he designed with the help of his assistant. The client dealt directly with the principal and the principal dealt directly with his assistant. Today a hierarchical structure has been forced upon this situation with as many as three levels of partners and associates, with senior assistants, assistants and technicians plus, of course, librarians, secretaries, typists and print boys.

The greatly increased running costs of the larger offices and the ever-pressing need for more work mean that the principals must concentrate on 'job getting'. Once the job has been acquired, the principal slips into the background, and the client finds himself working with a partner or associate and his commission designed by an assistant. Thus the architect–client relationship, already impaired by the former's difficulties in mastering an expanding technology, is now fragmented by the impersonal organization of the larger practices.

The big practice in its present form, although economically viable and able to provide a satisfactory building design service, is doomed to failure as it cannot provide the personal relationship which is at the crux of its existence as a professional organization. This concept of professionalism among those who design buildings has developed over a period of about six hundred years and some believe that it is time for a change. From this belief has come the package deal company. The package deal is in part the answer to the information explosion. It eliminates a large part of the information transference by combining in one organization the design and building teams, while offering the client only solutions which fit the previous experience, available resources and existing commitments of the company. By these means maximum economy is obtained by minimizing the design effort, while at the same time continuity of output for all sections of the organization is provided as far as is possible. From the client's point of view it has all the advantages of the Model-T. Ford. Traditionally, the building industry has supplied a large percentage of the nation's building directly to clients without recourse to an architect. In many respects the package deal company is only continuing this practice, except that the modern requirements of planning regulation and, to a lesser extent design, have required that they employ qualified architects. The danger to the profession inherent in this situation stems from the fact that with modern means of advertising at their disposal, the package dealers could deliberately complete the destruction of that relationship which the architects have themselves so seriously undermined.

One way out of this possible catastrophe is for the architect to re-shape his practice to provide first an office structure orientated to the needs of the client, and second a more expert and coherent total design service. The remainder of this book is concerned with how computers could aid such a reshaping; but first it is necessary to explain briefly how an electronic digital computer is used.

2 THE COMPUTER

2.1 Logic and Operation

Commercial computers are now quite common, and most people have seen one or at least have seen a photograph of a computer room. A typical installation consists of a number of separate cabinets of various shapes, including some obviously recognizable machines such as magnetic tape units and usually a teletype writer. The most uninteresting-looking of the cabinets is a plain rectangular box without any dials or lights. This is the actual computer or *Central Processing Unit* (CPU), which contains circuits which manipulate the electronic pulses by which the system operates, adding or subtracting them so as to carry out the calculations required. Every calculation consists of processes which can be reduced to addition and subtraction and the working of a computer is totally dependent upon this fact. The other items making up the computer installation are *peripherals*.

A peripheral does one of three things or a combination of two. It can provide a means of inputting information to the computer or a means of extracting it, or it can provide a means of storing the information. More will be said about peripherals later.

The computer's capacity to solve a problem by means of complex patterns of addition and subtraction is totally dependent upon the problem being fully understood, so that the exact sequence of events for obtaining a solution can be written down in a form which the computer can follow. The planning of such a sequence in a totally logical way to suit a computer is called programming, and the resulting plan a *program*, this spelling being now universally accepted. To plan a complex calculation solely in terms of instructions to add and subtract is a very tedious operation. Therefore, as the sequence of events required to, for instance, multiply, or obtain a cube root is the same every time it is used, it is clearly sensible to determine all the mathematical functions before starting and provide a means of specifying which is required by a code. This code is called a *programming language* and each language requires a *program language compiler* which is fed to the CPU before any program using the language. The 'higher' the language, the easier it is write a program but the bigger the compiler, and there is therefore less space in the CPU for calculation. Each computer also requires a *system program* which relates all the peripherals to the CPU so that the program can include instructions to bring automatically any combination of the available machines into operation, and feed information between them. This also must be stored in the CPU.

It is important to remember the amount of work which has gone into preparing the system program and compiler, as it accounts for the apparently human, even superhuman capacity the computer appears to have when operating. To the uninitiated watching a computer in action, the capacity the machine appears to possess to answer a question or, for example, to propose a course of action when a program does not operate correctly, is quite uncanny. In fact the questions and answers have all been foreseen by the designers of the system program and compiler during what was probably the many man-years of effort which went into preparing them.

Once a computer has a system program which operates it and a language compiler which makes it convenient to write programs, any reasonably intelligent person can make use of it to solve problems which he understands. To do so, however, he must learn the language. FORTRAN and ALGOL are the names of the two high-level languages at present best suited to most architectural problems.[3]

Most schoolboys now know that computers do not work with decimal numbers but with binary, and they also know that the reason for this is the simplicity of registering the two options which binary requires. With decimals, each digit has ten alternatives—0 to 9—but with binary there are only two, 0 and 1, and this can be represented by, for example, a very small spot on a magnetic tape. If the spot when checked is unmagnetized the reading is zero; if it is magnetized the reading is 1.

From this very simple beginning it is possible to compute the path of a rocket going to the moon and many other much more complex operations.

Handling millions of small magnetic spots requires organization, and the first step towards this is to group them into *words*. A computer word normally consists of six, twelve, eighteen, twenty-four or thirty-six spots or binary digits (bits) which are never separated. Each group can be used to represent numbers or letters of the alphabet, and words are combined when one is not large enough to represent the number to be stored.

The programmer specifies the maximum value which can possibly occur for each number arising in the operation of the program, and the compiler automatically allocates the number of words required. Each word or group of words so allocated is called an *operand* and has to be given a reference, so that when the value it is intended to hold becomes available its location (on the magnetic tape for example) is known, and when the value is needed again, it can be found and read. This reference is called the *address*. It is, of course, the operating program which ensures that the operand can be located or read and it is the compiler which provides the format for addressing.

To write a computer program it is necessary to understand a language, but it is not necessary to know very much about the computer and it is quite unnecessary to know anything about electronics. The architect who uses a computer can learn a language or he can depend upon a programmer to write it for him from flowcharts which the architect has prepared.

26

Though obviously the last process is a more expensive way of preparing material than writing it oneself, it does have the advantage that the final program can be prepared in the most appropriate language, i.e. not just the one the architect knows. Also, of course, the programmer is an expert, so the process should be considerably faster and more efficiently done, and could well prove cheaper if the architect's own time is costed.

It is essential that any architect wishing to design a computer program should be able to prepare flowcharts. Except in the case of very simple problems, the flowchart is the only practical way to define the logical solution of a problem and describe it to the programmer. It is very rare for a computer program to require mathematics of any complexity. School A-Level maths is normally quite sufficient. To design programs requires above all else a logical mind.

The computer is a machine capable of very high-speed computations, and this is its main value. It not only reduces the drudgery associated with long and repetitive calculations, but makes possible the solution of problems which can be conceived but which it would be quite impractical to solve by normal hand calculation. Man, however, can often solve problems which are beyond the capacity of the computer. The computer knows only logic and cannot, like man, use intuition, at least not yet.

2.2 The CPU and Peripherals

The Central Processing Unit (CPU) consists of three sections: a *Controller* which examines the program instructions one after the other and directs the action of the computer; the *Arithmetic Unit* which performs the addition and subtraction; and *Core Store* where the system program, compiler, program and data about to be operated upon are stored.

The Controller allocates part of the Core Store for the holding of data being processed by the Arithmetic Unit. When the processing is over and the program moves on to the next step, the Controller will transfer the data to other storage devices and bring in from them the fresh data required. Ideally, all the data required for a particular program would be held in the Core, as information from within it is almost instantly accessible. However, Core Store is expensive, so peripherals are used which store data by other means.

The peripheral storage, or *backing store* as it is called, is of several types and in general its cost is inversely proportional to the speed with which it can be accessed by the processor. Each computer therefore normally possesses a hierarchy of storage systems, each lower layer having a larger and larger capacity but, of course, being increasingly slower to access.

Transfer from Core Store to the processor is normally measured in micro seconds. The fastest type of backing store is the

8, 9
An *ICL System* 4 Computer

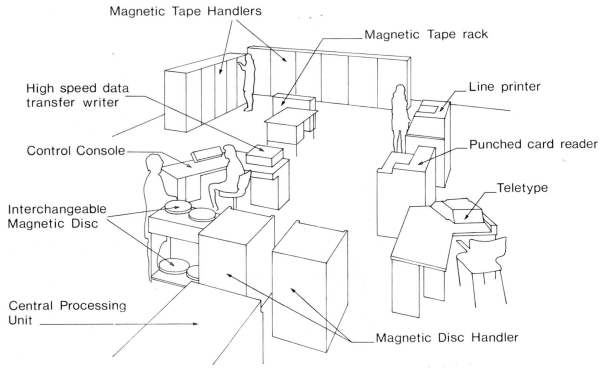

Magnetic Tape Handlers

Magnetic Tape rack

High speed data transfer writer

Line printer

Control Console

Punched card reader

Interchangeable Magnetic Disc

Teletype

Central Processing Unit

Magnetic Disc Handler

10
Control Console with teletype writer

11
High speed data transfer writer

12
Line printer

13
Magnetic tape handler

14
Punched card reader

15
Magnetic disc handler

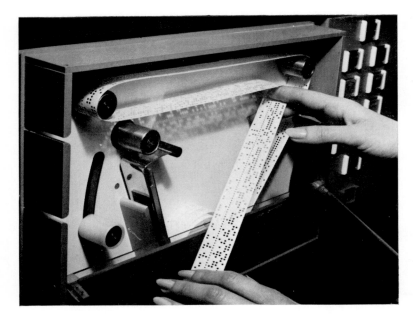

magnetic drum or disc, both of which consist of magnetic surfaces, of the shape suggested by the names, which are kept spinning continuously at high speed. Reading heads are arranged so that every part of the magnetic surface can be accessed in a revolution and transferred to the Core in a few milliseconds. The drum normally has the larger capacity, but the discs can be interchanged like records on a player, so that a single disc handler has a much greater capacity as long as information is not required simultaneously from two discs.

Magnetic tape is the next level. Information can be read from a tape at a similar speed to that of magnetic disc or drum, but whereas all the information on a disc or drum is immediately accessible, with tape a search process is required along the length of it to find the point of storage and this may take seconds or even minutes.

The lowest level of automatic information reading device is the paper tape or card reader, both of which are much slower and store binary information as small holes punched in the paper.

Although the punched paper tape and cards are methods of storage of information, unlike the magnetic storage techniques they are not suitable for use as an integral part of a program as methods of reading from them are too slow. Their ideal use is as an input device. The program and data can be prepared most easily for reception by the computer using a card or tape punching machine, and the inputting of the program and data at the beginning of the program can with some machines take place when the central processor is otherwise engaged. Punched

30

cards are particularly useful for data input during programming as they can be easily prepared and small changes made as the program is developed.

The slowest method of data input used on a computer is by teletype, where a human operator types instructions and a similar automatic output is obtained from the computer. Such a procedure is normally only used for very limited information.

The photograph of the computer installation at the beginning of this chapter includes a conventional teletype on the right-hand side, while in the centre of the picture is an alternative high-speed input/output writer. Mounted on the same desk is a central control console from which the operation of the computer can be monitored. Many early computers were controlled almost entirely from the teletype, but most modern machines have this more direct control which is particularly important when the machine is operating in a *time-sharing* mode. Time-sharing is the technique of handling a number of programs or processes simultaneously, while the computer automatically manipulates them between the CPU and the backing store.

The program is normally designed to output the results of the calculation so that they can be read directly. The teletype can be used for this if the quantity involved is not too great, but otherwise a line printer is more commonly used. A line printer is similar to a teletype, but here an entire line of type is printed simultaneously by a multi-head device which provides a very high-speed printed output. When a very large quantity of information is to be outputted, special high-speed photographic printing devices can be used, but these are not yet common items in the computer room.

The operation of a typical program is approximately as follows. The program on punched card or punched paper tape is fed from a reader to the computer, the computer having been previously fed with its system program and program compiler, both of which are normally stored on magnetic tape. As the cards are fed in, the program compiler converts the program to the form the machine requires. When the program-compiling operation is complete, a request to proceed is printed out automatically on the teletype. At this point the data for the particular problem is fed in also via one of the readers and is stored either in the Core Store or—if the quantity is great—upon a disc or magnetic tape, from where it will be transferred to the Core Store in sections by the controller as required. The program will then proceed to carry out the calculations, and when these are complete the results will appear in the form specified by the program, usually on the line printer.

The operation of a typical commercial computer is somewhat easier than driving a car, and no architect should have any serious difficulty in understanding or using one. The biggest obstruction to a greater understanding of computer techniques by those outside the computer industry is the massive new terminology it has been found necessary to invent in order that the initiated can communicate. Anyone wishing to make use of a computer must master a basic knowledge of this terminology, and for this purpose a computer dictionary is to be strongly recommended.[4]

2.3 Computer Graphics

With many calculations the results are best illustrated in a graphic form, and for this purpose a number of methods have been developed whereby the output of a program can be presented directly by the computer drawing a graph or diagram. Such techniques all depend upon an ability to describe a drawing in digital form which can be stored in the computer and manipulated by it.

This is normally done by a coding system whereby the operator describes each line upon the drawing in terms of the coordinates at the ends of the line and the shape the line possesses. This code can be stored and programs written which will treat the code as information for computation purposes, re-draw the drawing as output or make modifications to it and re-draw the modified version. This outputting is normally carried out using a *plotter*.

Plotters come in various forms but consist always of some type of draughting pointer such as a pen, pencil, biro or beam of light, and a mechanical system which directs the pointer from the one digitised position to the other along a shape specified by the code. The cheapest of these machines consists of a drum on which the paper is mounted, while the pointer is on a gantry above the length of the drum. The rotation of the drum provides motion in one direction, and the movement of the pointer along the gantry the motion in the other direction. By this means a normal two-dimensional drawing can be constructed upon a sheet of paper on the drum.

17
A small, twelve-inch drum plotter by Calcomp Ltd. This machine is also available for paper widths of 30 and 36 inches

A more expensive type of plotter is the *flat bed plotter* in which the gantry is supported on a second system of bearings along which it is driven so as to produce motion in two dimensions over a flat surface. Here the sheet is laid flat upon a bed as the name suggests, and the construction of the drawing can be easily followed while the computer is in operation.

Various techniques can be used to obtain the original coding of the drawing. The drawing can be made by hand on squared paper and the coordinates taken off from the squares and code numbers developed from them and from the shape of the line. A much faster and more satisfactory technique is to use a *digitiser*. A digitiser normally consists of a drawing-board to which is attached a movable head consisting of a cross-hair and magnifying glass. This head can be moved over the drawing,

18
A Kingmatic flat bed plotter with off-line magnetic-tape control unit made by Kongsberg Vapenfabrik A/S, Norway

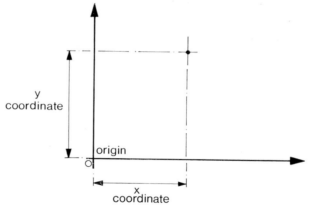

A position defined in two dimensions by cartesian coordinates

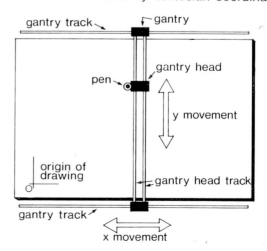

19
Action of plotter is derived from cartesian coordinate geometry, as used in everyday graph plotting. Horizontal movement of gantry over board provides changes in x coordinate, and vertical movement of head, along the gantry provides changes in y coordinate. An up-and-down movement of the pen controls whether or not a line is drawn on the paper

Operating Principle of a Flat Bed Plotter

A C—C

20
A D-Mac Ltd. low-cost digitising
board. The principle is similar to
that of the flat bed plotter, except
that the head and gantry are
moved by hand to position the
cross-hair over the location to be
digitised

positioned accurately over any spot, and at a press of a button
the position of the spot is registered. The position of the cross-
hairs at the moment the button is pressed can be measured in a
number of different ways. One simple method is to have the
cross-hair, magnifier and button on a mounting attached to a
gantry over the board along with a pair of devices, one of
which will record the position of the gantry as it is slid sideways
across the board, while the other will record the position of the
mounting as it slides up and down the gantry. Such a system
will register the position of the cross-hair as two coordinates,
the x measurement being that of the position of the gantry,
and the y being the position of the mounting upon the gantry,
each coordinate being measured from an arbitrarily specified
origin at the bottom left corner of the board.

A program can be prepared which will result in the computer
storing the x and y coordinates each time the button is
pressed, and relating them in pairs as being the two ends of a
line. If, in addition, a code word is added with the coded
coordinates which specify the shape of the line, then entire
drawings can be coded to be read back and reconstructed at a
later date. Programs are available, of course, for each digitiser
which permits this type of information to be prepared, and for
each plotter to permit it to be re-read and the drawing produced automatically.

A lot of work has also been done in the field of computer
graphics using *Cathode-Ray Tubes* (CRT). The CRT offers a
means of displaying information which is stored in the Core in
a graphic form. Once displayed, a drawing can be modified by
means of the so-called *light pen*. The pen, which is in fact
more a pointer, is used to indicate objects on the screen, to
move them around, or to pin-point positions to which they are
to be moved. It is this technique of assembling already digi-

21
An ICL Cathode ray-tube display
and light pen. The operator is
modifying a housing layout produced by the BAID program (see
Chapter 6).

tised objects which has proved to be the light pen's principal purpose.

The electronics required to operate a cathode-ray tube and light pen are very expensive. This, plus the fact that few people wish to spend more than two hours a day working close to a large cathode-ray tube, limits the potential of this equipment for the architect.

A much cheaper device is the *Direct View Storage Tube*. The DVST or storage tube is similar in appearance and action to a cathode-ray tube, but the coating on the inside of the tube can be covered by a negative charge into which lines can be 'cut' using a high-power positive electron beam. The screen is then flooded with a low-power positive electron beam which causes the coating of the tube to display the image cut by the high-power beam. The picture can be erased by simply recharging the screen negatively. The action of cutting the outline to be displayed is carried out by one sweep of the high-power beam, so that the image can be inspected without using the electronics to continuously refurbish it as is required with a cathode-ray display.

A storage tube is thus ideal for sustaining a static image while the information on it is studied. It is not, however, suited to show motion, although some degree of movement can be effected by rapid replacement of the image. As yet, no equivalent to the light pen has been developed for the storage tube, but it is possible by means of a joy stick to move a small spot of light over the screen and this can be used as a pointer. The simplicity and relatively low cost of the storage tube and the steady image it sustains means that it is of great interest to those concerned with low-cost computer graphics.

2.4 The Bureau

The *Computer Bureau* is a company which operates one or more computers on a multi-access system. That is to say the computers are themselves controlled by a machine which feeds to them data received from a number of different sources. By this means the CPU of each of the bureau's machines can be kept operating to give them maximum output.

The input of data can come from cubicles at the bureau, in each of which is an input device such as a teletype, or it can come via telex or telephone line. The input is stored briefly until a CPU is available, then processed and the results returned to the operator. The user pays a processing charge for the computer time and a hire charge for the cubicle or the input terminal he has at the other end of the line. The processing charge varies depending upon the degree of priority requested. For most architectural design problems, the lowest degree of priority should be satisfactory, namely overnight batch processing. For the regular user, it is logical to hire a terminal.

22
A Tektronix Ltd. storage tube. The tube can be used in either vertical or horizontal format

23
A Datadynamics Ltd. teletype writer with paper tape punch and reader. This is the basic machine used on most computers and bureau terminals

There are a number of different types of terminal which vary in their speed of operation and the type of line they use. The fastest terminals require private telephone lines and the running costs involved are only justified if the computer is to be used on a large scale. At the other end of the scale there is a terminal called a MODEM, which uses an STD telephone line. This terminal is cheap to hire but slow to use. Only the input data and output results need be transmitted via the terminal; the program can be retained by the bureau so the terminal limitations relate to the amount of data used and not the size of the program. The computer bureau provides a convenient means for the small architectural practice to use a large computer, and we are likely to see many terminals installed in the next decade. In the following chapter, the possible uses of a terminal will be discussed more fully.

2.5 Programming and Flowcharts

Before a problem can be conveniently programmed, it must first be described in flowchart form. To write the program from the flowchart does not then require the programmer to have any detailed knowledge of the problem. The preparation of the flowchart, however, should be carried out by a person expert in the subject with which the problem is concerned.

The complete flowchart of a large program is not constructed as one massive chart, but as many small charts which are grouped together into higher level charts through several stages. Thus the program can be described in a single chart, which consists of a diagram where each step is an entire sub-program in itself, while each sub-program is detailed on a separate chart. Often each sub-program will also break down into a series of smaller sub-programs. It is regarded as desirable that each final sub-program should be small enough to fit on a single page. By this means each page can be checked without reference to any other, so minimizing the risk of error.

The method used to construct flowcharts is quite simple and a brief study of the basic techniques will give the reader an insight into the way in which computer programs work, and should assist in his understanding of the remainder of this book.

The first figure shows the symbols used when constructing a flowchart. A flowchart consists of a series of boxes the shape of which indicates the type of operation described within it; the lines connecting the boxes and the arrows upon them indicate the direction of flow between the various operations.

The diamond-shaped box forms the basic operation and indicates the 'yes' or 'no' decision which the operation must decide. Such decisions are normally of the form does A = B?, or is A greater than B? The answer must be either 'yes' or 'no' and the diamond always has two paths departing from it, one labelled 'yes' and the other 'no'. The rectangular box indicates any processing operation other than a decision. Such operations often occur as a result of a decision and consist of a direction to the computer to proceed to a particular calculation or to give a certain value to a stated parameter. The trapezoidal box indicates an input or output operation, and an oval box is the beginning or end point of a program or sub-program.

Two small flowcharts are now described to illustrate first how a calculation can be made, and second how a simple geometrical relationship can be investigated. Such charts do not, of course, in themselves represent a whole computer program but only a very small sub-program.

The First Flowchart:

If an architect were to use a computer to plan a housing layout, it is likely that at various stages of the work he would wish to know how many dwellings of each size had been so far used and the percentage of each size represented.

Let us assume, without going into detail at this stage, that he is planning with a light pen on a CRT and that he has an option of dwelling sizes, each of which has either 2, 3, 4, or 5 rooms. The principal program which aids in the planning will provide some facility whereby the designer can display a new dwelling on the screen and move it into position with the light pen. As he introduces the new dwelling, the computer will automatically give it a number N and note the size R specified, namely the number of rooms the new dwelling is to have ($R = 2, 3, 4$ or 5). The designer can specify his choice for R in a number of ways. The simplest, for example, is to arrange for the computer to put a dwelling on the screen when either of the keys 2, 3, 4 or 5 on the teletype keyboard is depressed. At any stage in the process, the program could print out on the teletype the number and percentage of each dwelling type used, and it could do this once the designer had depressed the key marked '%'. In order to carry out this last procedure, the program would need to include a sub-program as follows:

24
Flowchart Symbols

A decision, each line leaving the box must be labelled with a decision, the result of which causes the path to be followed

An operation other than a decision

Input or output

Beginning or end of a program

Every line must have an arrow indicating the direction of flow

The depression of the key marked '%' on the teletype will result

① in the program first reading into an allocated part of the Core Store all the values of N and the corresponding values of R in the order in which they have been introduced, and the value of T, where T is the total number of dwellings so far used. It will also

② clear to zero, registers allocated to store values of D2, D3, D4, D5 and P2, P3, P4 and P5 which may have residual results left over from a previous use. D2, D3, etc., are variables which at any point in the computation represent the number of 2-, 3-, 4- and 5-roomed dwellings so far dealt with, while P2, P3, etc., are the corresponding percentages of each type. In the case of P2 for example,

$$P2 = \frac{D2 \times 100}{T}.$$

The value of N is then

③ made equal to 1 and the first value R checked to discover whether it is 2, 3, 4 or 5. This is done in the way shown in the chart first

④ by checking if it is equal to 2 then

⑤ if it is equal to 3 and then

⑥ if equal to 4. Whenever the answer is 'yes', the flow causes the program to pass through an operation which increases the corresponding value of D by 1. This is written $D = D + 1$. After each such check, the value of N is similarly checked

⑦ to see if it equals T, and if not

⑧ then N is increased by 1 which results in the next value of R in the list being checked. When finally N does equal T, the route changes through the flowchart,

⑨ and the values for P2, P3, P4 and P5 are calculated. All the required values are then printed out

⑩. Such a program, if operated on a medium sized computer of the type required to back up a CRT and light pen, would perform this check for a hundred dwellings in about 0·5 seconds, excluding the print-out which on a teletype would take about 1·5 seconds.

The Second Flowchart:

This chart is part of a program which investigates the inter-relationship of dwellings on a site. A simple example has been chosen where a dwelling H is assumed to have a view in the direction shown, and the object is to check the locations of other possible dwellings so as to eliminate any which obstruct the view of H. This could be one of a series of checks in a program to design, say, an arrangement of holiday villas which claim an unobstructed view of the sea. What constitutes obstruction is, of course, open to question. However, for the purpose of this exercise, it has been assumed that if a person

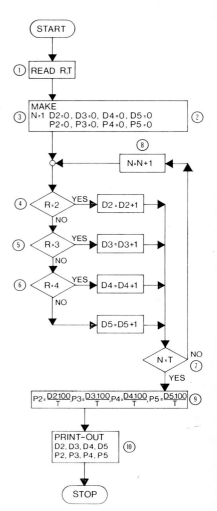

25
First Flowchart

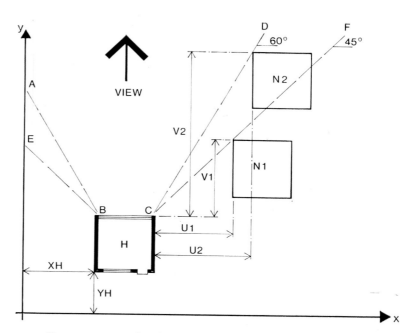

standing at any point behind the fully glazed front BC of the dwelling can see another dwelling within his central angle of vision of sixty degrees (i.e. thirty degrees either side of the centre), then the view is obstructed; or alternatively, if more than one dwelling falls within an angle of ninety degrees (forty-five degrees either side of centre), then this also will constitute an obstruction. The significance of the angles is not just to the view of someone standing immediately behind the glass. If a wide-angled view is clear at this point, then someone positioned at a point further back in the room will not be able to see any obstructions.

Thus, if a second dwelling N is positioned so that no part of it obstructs the view of H, it must lie entirely outside the area ABCD; and if all the dwellings from N = 1 to N = T are checked, only one may protrude into the area between ABCD and EBCF. For the purposes of this exercise, it is assumed that all dwellings are square, and have a side length equal to L. The first move ① on the second chart is to make N = 1 and I = 0, where I is an indicator which will show whether the intermediate zone between ABCD and EBDF has yet its one permissible obstruction.

As shown in the diagram with the second chart, for the purposes of designing the program the dwellings are seen as plotted upon a graph, so the position of each is described by the coordinates of the bottom left-hand corner of the dwelling. The second operation ② in the chart is to determine the values XH, YH, L and T, followed by ③ the first values of XN and YN.

Clearly any position of dwelling N for which YH is greater than YN ④ will mean that the new location is alongside or behind the dwelling H. This can be listed immediately as satisfactory ⑥ from the point of view of dwelling H. If, however, dwelling N is in front of dwelling H, then each zone must be checked. Take as an example the dwelling N1 which is on the edge of the outer zone EBCF. Clearly, since CF is at an angle of forty-five degrees, the dwelling will be outside the zone if $U1 > V1$;

but

$$V1 = YN - YH$$

and

$$U1 = (XN - XH) - L$$

so

$$(XN - X1) - L > YN - YH$$

A check on the other side against the line EB produces the same equation except that

$$U1 = (XH - XN) - L$$

In each case the positive difference (i.e. the absolute value) of $(XH - XN)$ is required, otherwise the equation is the same and this value is used ⑤ in the flowchart. If the dwelling does not protrude into the zone EBCF, the position is accepted, ⑥ the value of N checked ⑦ against T, and if the two are not equal N increased ⑧ by 1 and the next position checked. If it does protrude, however, the next move ⑨ is to check whether or not any part of it extends into the inner zone ABCD. Here again the equation is similar, but as in the case of dwelling N2 the angle is sixty degrees, we have to check $U2 . \tan 60° > V2$ or

$$\sqrt{2} \, [\text{abs} \, (XH - XN) - L] > YN - YH$$

If the answer this time is 'no', the dwelling N2 must be between the two zones. It will therefore be acceptable if it is the first to be so placed. The value of I is then checked ⑩. If I equals 0 then I is made equal to 1, and the dwelling is accepted. If I is found ⑪ already to equal 1, then the dwelling is rejected. The dwelling is also rejected, of course, if the answer to the previous operation was 'yes', because if the value of the last equation above shows that $U2 . \tan 60°$ is not greater than V2, then the dwelling N2 must protrude into the inner zone ABCD which is impermissible. After a ⑫ rejection, N is checked ⑦ against T and if it is found not to equal it, N is increased by 1 and the next dwelling checked. When N equals T, the program prints out the results and stops.

These two simple flowcharts both illustrate the use of a

loop by means of which a program can cycle through a list of values in the process of determining a required answer. This technique is basic to programming, as most operations performed by a flowchart are individually quite simple and the power of a computer lies in the capacity to perform such operations in large numbers and at great speed.

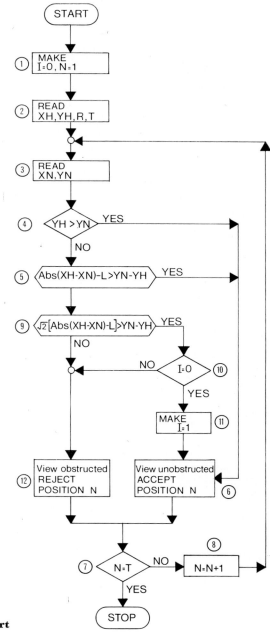

27
Second Flowchart

3 THE DESIGN OFFICE COMPUTER

3.1 The Computer Market

The computers discussed in the last chapter were initially developed for either research computation or commercial accounting, and the fact that they have proved suitable for design has been largely coincidental. The size of these machines, however, puts them outside the scope of all but a few very large professional offices—not only because of their cost, but also their capacity, which is far greater than any small office could utilize for more than a few minutes every day. Thus it is that the aircraft industry, with its large resources and centralized design offices, has led the way in the development of computer-aided design, while the professions concerned with the building industry have followed more cautiously behind. At present, the computer bureaux provide the simplest means of access to a large computer for most professional engineering offices for such work as structural design and duct-flow analysis, and could serve in a similar way for design computation in architecture.

With architectural design, it is questionable whether the use of such machines is at present economically viable in the context of the architect's scale of fees and the cost of design by normal methods. The running cost of these machines has fallen steadily however for some years, and we can be reasonably certain that by the second half of this decade this problem will have been overcome. In the last five years a new low-cost computer market has developed in the field of process control which has unexpected interest for the profession.

The process control computer is basically an instrument for automation, and although each manufacturer predicts the widest scope for his products, he expects a major part of his output to be used on the factory floor. These machines are therefore robust, do not require air-conditioning and are generally cheap. The same holds true for the peripheral equipment with which they operate. Originally these machines were generally small and were intended to be pre-set for many repetitions of the same operation. They have, however, developed rapidly and now offer all the original advantages plus greatly increased power and flexibility at prices which have in some cases more than halved since the model was originally introduced. This type of computer is capable of operating a digitiser and plotter effectively, and with a compatible low-cost system of information storage on magnetic tape, a system virtually exists for storing and reproducing graphic information of the type with which the architect deals in his daily work.

This is, of course, a different situation to that visualized with the Bureau Computer. Here, when a problem arises, it is solved rapidly by the use of a program which has been designed for that particular problem. The process control computer on the other hand needs to be in constant use in the process of

43

information collection and transformation—which as we have seen is the basic problem in the architect's office. For this purpose the computer must be in the office, which is quite conceivable as it is a low-cost machine.

The problem of the potential cost of a practical system is paramount. Computers are rarely bought; they are hired at a yearly rate which includes maintenance and which is chargeable against tax. Because of the wide range of machines available, it is always possible to improve a system by spending more, so it is impractical to design without a particular target in mind. In the case of the system described in the next chapter, a budget of £20,000 ($44,000) has been aimed at. This is equivalent to a yearly hire charge corresponding approximately to the total cost of one additional assistant, and should allow any office considering the installation of such a system to estimate from experience what the system must provide in order to be worth the expenditure.

3.2 The PDP- 8/e Computer

The process control computer market has expanded rapidly in the last two years and several small machines have become available which could be used in a system of the type to be described. For the purposes of this book, however, we will consider one typical computer of this type, namely the PDP-8/e made by The Digital Equipment Corporation of America and The Digital Equipment Co. Ltd., England.

The PDP-8/e is a rectangular box, 24 inches deep, with a front panel 19 inches wide × 10½ inches high. Within this box is the CPU and a Core Store memory of 4000–12 bit words (4K words), which can be expanded in blocks of 4K up to 32K words, all of which fit inside the box. The front panel is a control console on which are 21 toggle switches, a panel lock and a six-position control switch. Each toggle has an indicator lamp and 12 of the switches and lamps group together in the switch register to make up a single computer word.

28
A PDP/8e computer in desk top form. Digital Equipment Corporation

The toggle switches allow a manual control of the computer and provide the most elementary means of transferring words into the Core Store. With the switches, the user can address a location in the Core Store and, by switching, display the contents of the location on the switch register. Likewise he can set a value on the switch register and transfer it to the location in the store previously set on the memory address register.

When the computer is switched to power by the key lock for the first time, the Core Store will be empty and inactive. The first action therefore must be to transfer into the core a simple program called a loader, which is a minimum program linking one of the peripherals to the computer so as to permit that peripheral to load further programs. The loader, which consists of ten instructions, is set up on the switch register by the toggle switches. To save time an optional hardware loader is available which fits inside the computer case and provides the same facility at the flick of a single switch. Once this is done, a short paper tape is fed into the core and this allows the main program to be read from either paper tape or magnetic tape. Once the program is loaded, the key is switched to panel lock and normally no further use is made of the panel switches unless a program modification is required. The operator working with a prepared set of programs and a hardware loader need know very little about the operation of the computer.

When a program is in use the passage of each step within it is marked by a flash of the switch register and memory address indicator lights. The operation of various loops in the program produces rhythmical patterns on the indicator light, a feature the reader should be familiar with if he has noticed the cockpit controls used in any recent Hollywood space epic. Although the significance of the patterns of light produced may be quite meaningless to the operator, with use he will tend to recognize the rhythms and patterns produced by the different types of programs and so spot one which is malfunctioning.

The PDP-8/e has a 12 bit word which can be combined in pairs to give the 24 bit double precision words required for draughting. With the core expanded to 8K, a useful FORTRAN compiler can be employed which permits small programs written in this language to be used. Greater efficiency of operation is achieved, however, and more core space is preserved for working if programs are written in a lower level language suited to this particular machine.

The ASR33 teletype console is the basic input/output device for the PDP-8/e. The keyboard can be operated as described above to input to the computer instructions, which are simultaneously typed on a paper roll. Mounted on the side of the ASR33 is a paper tape punch and reader, so that a simultaneous copy of what is typed can also be punched on tape in the 8-channel perforation code ASCII (American Standard

Code for Information Interchange). The computer can also output to the teletype and its tape punch, and the teletype can be switched to operate independently of the computer for production of punched paper tapes.

A range of other peripherals is available, including high-speed paper tape handlers, magnetic tape and disc handlers and many other devices which can be linked to the computer. One peripheral which is unique to this particular machine is the DECtape System. This consists of a compact magnetic tape reader, two of which fit a cabinet the same size as the computer. The tapes are of a special heavy gauge and appear, unlike normal magnetic tapes, to be unaffected by bad atmospheric conditions. The tape is on a small 4-inch diameter reel and has one unusual feature. Blocks of information on the tape can be directly addressed, unlike conventional magnetic tapes which have to be searched sequentially. This feature helps to reduce substantially the access time of the tape.

3.3 The CADMAC Digitiser-Plotter

Another very interesting advance in this field is represented by the CADMAC Digitiser-Plotter System developed by Colin Besant and Alan Jebb at the Imperial College of Science and Technology, London, in conjunction with D-Mac Limited who are now manufacturing a range of tables.[5] The system combines in one table the processes of digitising and plotting, so that a single set of electronics can be used for both. This system is comparable to a typical drum plotter for accuracy, which is of the order required for the production of most technical drawings.

The table consists of a flat box, the bottom of which is a drawing surface and the top a glass panel. Inside the box is the usual gantry of a flat bed plotter carrying a pen which writes upon paper mounted on the lower surface. Drawings to be

29
**A double DECtape handler.
Digital Equipment Corporation**

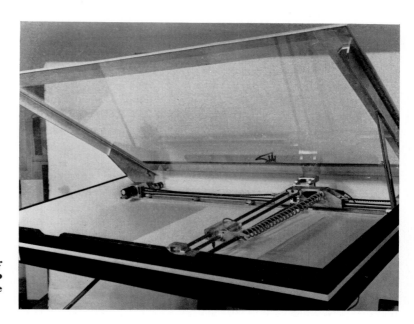

30
The Cadmac digitiser-plotter table. The glass top is open to show the gantry system and the plotting surface

31
The D-Mac Ltd. digitiser as used on the top surface of the Cadmac table

digitised are fixed to the top of the glass panel, and when the machine is switched to the digitising mode, the gantry head automatically follows the digitiser when the latter is moved over the drawing by the operator. It does this electromagnetically. The magnified cross-hair glass in the digitiser is surrounded by a coil which sets up a magnetic field which is monitored by three sensors mounted on the gantry head. When digitising is in progress, these sensors control the servo-motors which drive the gantry and gantry head, and are able to centre the head accurately under the digitiser cross-hair. The usual press-button action causes the position of the gantry head to be recorded. The digitiser is either in the form of a magnified cross-hair, or a pointer which can also be a ball pen. The position of the digitiser and gantry is registered by a digital display as x and y coordinates. This display can be connected directly to the table or via the computer which allows the values to be modified so as, for example, to display them to various scales. The gantry head is counter-balanced so that the digitising can be carried out with the table tilted to an angle to suit a seated operator.

At present this machine is available with a single pen head, although pens are interchangeable. Thus a ball pen, which is the most trouble-free type, can be used for general work. However, when a higher quality of line is required, a rapidograph type drawing ink pen can be employed. It is also practical to change pen sizes. Multi-pen heads are also available, which permit a range of pen sizes or colours to be used on a drawing without intervention of the operator for major parts of the drawing. This manual interchange of pens is not as convenient as the automatic multi-head type of plotter, but in practice the use of several ink pens is limited by the tendency of one to dry up while another is in use.

When digitising, it is not only necessary to specify the end coordinates of a line but also what type of line it is, continuous, broken, dotted, etc., and special routines are also required for different types of curved lines. For such operations, a separate panel of press buttons known as function key buttons can be linked into the system via the interface which relates the table either to an associated computer or a magnetic tape handler. An alternative is to allocate a narrow strip down one side of the working area of the digitising surface to a menu card. The menu card has areas drawn upon it which, when digitised, activate the required operation. This procedure has an advantage in that the operator can work for long periods with only the digitiser, and furthermore several hundred operations can be included on each menu card which can be interchangeable with the programs. The one disadvantage of the menu card technique is that for some operations which are used very frequently, it can be time-consuming and distracting to traverse the gantry to one extreme end of the table each time the operation is required. For such operations a small block of function buttons provides the logical approach, and digitising heads are available with a group of four or eight buttons mounted conveniently for use with either hand.

32
The pen head on the D-Mac plotter

The digitised positions are stored and re-drawn to the nearest 0·1 mm, with a maximum drawing length of 0·9999 m, so an A1 size drawing can be accepted with about 15 cm left over at one end for the menu card. The storage of four decimal digits requires a double precision 24 bit word, so each location is stored in two 24 bit words, one for each of the coordinates x and y.

3.4 Drawings and Schedules

When an architect provides a set of working drawings, specifications and schedules to a contractor for a traditionally constructed building, he tries to describe the work to be done fully enough for it to be built as he visualizes it. Much of the detailing of such a building, however, is dependent upon a mutual understanding between the architect and the craftsmen employed by the contractor. This is true of practically all industries which depend to some degree on personal skill, but it is particularly true of the building industry which has retained an unusually high proportion of genuine craft employment. As new building processes are introduced, the architect has to consider the information he provides against this background, and try to make the maximum use of the existing knowledge of the craftsmen so as to relate the new processes to the existing patterns, thus minimizing the area for misunderstandings.

The presentation of information in new ways is a similar situation, although here the individual architect faces a special problem. If he alone adopts a radically new system, unlike the engineer who is employed in the design office of a company, he cannot expect the extra expense involved in training operatives to understand his system to be recovered in the future, since he may not build again with this particular contractor for many years. Buildings, unlike any other designed objects, are nearly always related to an existing landscape which often includes other buildings, and this severely limits the degree of abstraction which can be employed when describing the construction and the degree of standardization possible in building. It is conceivable that a totally prefabricated building on a flat site could be described in a specification and the parts listed in a schedule so fully that working drawings would be unnecessary. Certain parts of buildings which traditionally require extensive drawing, in particular reinforced concrete structures, are now being detailed by some offices in this way. The specifications do, however, contain diagrams which in fact provide a minimal form of drawing.

For architectural design, it is impossible to dispense entirely with all forms of graphic presentation, and unless prefabrication with standard components is employed, extensive working drawings would appear to be inevitable. Early efforts to use computer aids in building often involved attempts to do without drawings, simply because adequate low cost computer graphics were not available.

For the practising architect, however, who may be involved in converting or extending existing structures as well as designing new ones, any office system must have universal or near universal application. Any computer aid to information handling which assumes the use of a certain type of construction or a certain range of prespecified components may prove to be totally irrelevant to the future projects an office acquires, unless that office is in the unusual situation of being able to refuse all but certain types of work. It is therefore the author's opinion that the only computer application which is likely to receive widespread acceptance is one in which the computer's resources are applied to the production of information which can describe the full range of building types and techniques which we are likely to be using in the near future. It follows that any such system must involve the production of scale drawings, not too dissimilar to those traditionally employed.

All working drawings are in fact sections. A section is an imaginary plane in space, and a drawing of it shows that which is cut by the plane and what appears behind it. Inclusion of too much information about the things behind the plane may obscure the section, so although as far as possible everything which is cut by the surface is shown, a decision regarding the

33

remainder is more arbitrary and must be judged against the information content.

Drawings of a vertical plane cutting through a building are actually called sections; drawings of horizontal planes are called plans and the vertical planes outside the building and parallel to one façade are called elevations. Parts of buildings and individual components can be similarly treated, and a long tradition exists for interpreting the meaning of this form of information presentation.

An architect's working drawings are each drawn to one of a fixed range of scales. Plans, sections and elevations are drawn to small scales so that they fit conveniently on a sheet, then details chosen from them are prepared to larger scales to show the construction to be used. For the remainder of this book, the plans, sections and elevations which are drawings of sections through an entire building or a major part of one will be called *Major Sections*, and the larger scale drawings which show individual components or groups of components will be called *Details*. In the discussion which follows of the principles behind a computer-aided draughting system, it is assumed that the graphic descriptions of buildings stored in such a system will be in the form of pre-chosen two-dimensional major sections. It might appear more logical, since buildings are three-dimensional, to store a single three-dimensional computer model of a project and thus be free to choose one's final sections at will by 'cutting' the model at any point.

Another advantage of this approach would be the capacity to compute quantities automatically as all the dimensions of every item in the building can be defined. It is possible that such a technique will one day be developed, but at present it appears that the volume of storage required and the amount of preparatory work involved is so immense as to make it quite impractical. The idea is nevertheless very attractive, and it is worth looking at a way in which it might be done in order the better to appreciate the problems involved.

The most likely way to define a building in space is to define the extremities of a rectangular volume into which the building will just fit, and then divide the volume into modular cubes and specify the contents of each cube. If the cube size relates to a building module and a dimensional standard, many of the cube faces will coincide with surfaces within the building. Bemis and Burchard first proposed this approach in their remarkable book *The Evolving House*, published in New York in 1936.[6] They illustrated a house (Fig. 34) so divided into 4-inch cubes. They chose a 4-inch module in order to relate to the 4×2 stud and 8-inch concrete blocks which were then the principal building materials for houses in the United States.

The 4-inch or 100-mm module has since become a recognized standard for dimensional coordination in Europe. Obviously

34
The house structure defined within the matrix from *The Evolving House*, by Bemis and Burchard

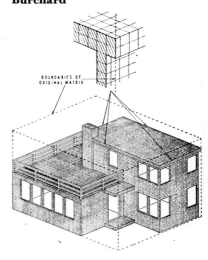

many of the cubes within such a volume will consist of nothing but air, but if an attempt is made to specify only cubes containing building materials, then each cube used must be located in three dimensions. If, however, the entire rectilinear volume is specified, the addressing of the information in the store can in itself specify the position within the volume. Whichever way is used, however, it would appear likely that the storage involved would be excessive. For example, a simple block of fifty apartments would require about ten million cubes to be defined. Just to specify the contents of each cube would be a big task, and yet in order to produce drawings it would appear necessary not only to define the contents but also the appearance of four or five of the faces.

With surprisingly little training, the average person can be taught to relate sections in order to visualize a three-dimensional space, and it is by this means that we transmit most information by drawing. The power and economy of this method is such that it seems unlikely that we will change very greatly the form in which we present information, and the same is probably true of our future methods of storing it.

3.5 Theory of a System

If a computer system is introduced into a private office, it must become productive at the earliest possible moment. It is not therefore practical to contemplate an extensive pre-production session in which a mass of input information is first introduced to the system. The architect's system should be operative almost from the first day, possibly as a mere alternative means for producing drawings. Then, as the operator builds up the computer's memory with information, so increasingly he will be able to draw upon the machine's developing capacity.

Several systems have been developed using larger computers to reproduce details of industrialized building systems and assemble them as required into designs. With a limited number of standard items, it has been found practical to store each item in great detail including all costings so that a project can be priced by the computer from the design.

This is a very attractive proposition, but it is impractical if the products are traditional since the numbers involved are too high, and many factors including price would be out of date before all but a few of them were applied. The architect using such a system for a wide range of varying products must work in terms of the minimum information which will serve his purpose, so that it remains relevant for as long as possible. By minimizing input, the time required to digitise the detail is kept to a few minutes, so there should be no in-built tendency not to revise the detail or introduce a new one as required.

When the sketch stage of the design is complete, the major sections required to illustrate the scheme can be chosen and the

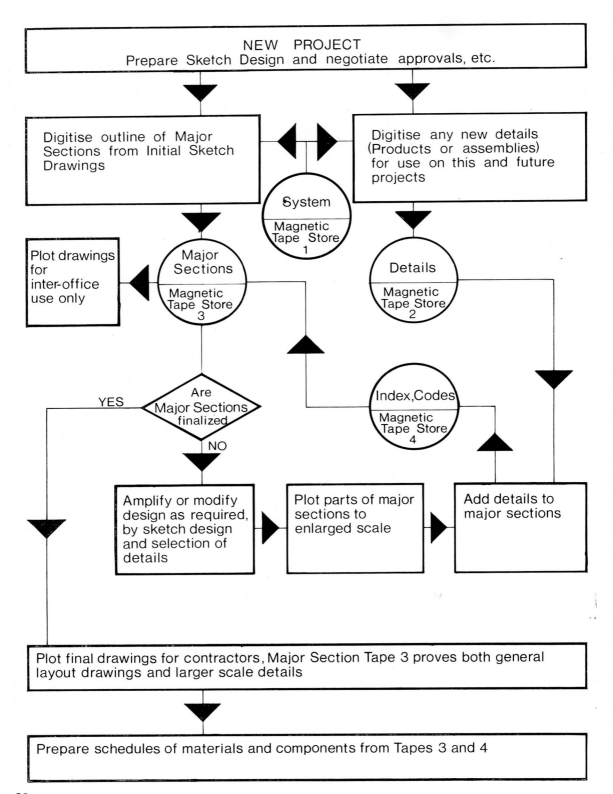

NEW PROJECT
Prepare Sketch Design and negotiate approvals, etc.

Digitise outline of Major Sections from Initial Sketch Drawings

Digitise any new details (Products or assemblies) for use on this and future projects

System
Magnetic Tape Store 1

Plot drawings for inter-office use only

Major Sections
Magnetic Tape Store 3

Details
Magnetic Tape Store 2

Are Major Sections finalized

YES

NO

Index, Codes
Magnetic Tape Store 4

Amplify or modify design as required, by sketch design and selection of details

Plot parts of major sections to enlarged scale

Add details to major sections

Plot final drawings for contractors, Major Section Tape 3 proves both general layout drawings and larger scale details

Prepare schedules of materials and components from Tapes 3 and 4 outline of each digitised. This will probably be done on a small-scale drawing, but the information stored is to full-scale. These major sections will provide a means of rapidly producing drawings of the bare outlines for studies involving planning, structure or services, etc. As each detail is decided, the area of the building affected can be selected from the appropriate major sections, enlarged, and the details added at the enlarged scale. All will, of course, be stored at the same scale, i.e. full size. These details can either be digitised by a drawing made by hand on top of the enlarged part of the major section, or they can be previously prepared to a standard which is copied from the computer's store of these standard items into the major sections' store. In this way a major section is fully detailed, and when complete can be reproduced entirely or in part to any scale within the limits of the table.

By coding each item drawn on the section, it is also possible to reproduce major sections in terms of one or more materials only. The same codes permit all the items drawn to be automatically scheduled. The following two chapters describe in more detail how such a system works using a PDP-8/e computer, CADMAC Digitiser-Plotter and a TEKTRONIX 611 Storage Tube which monitors results and displays options.

Such a system also provides a comprehensive terminal when combined with a modem. Thus, when the operator becomes fully adept at operating the system, its power can be extended to that of a large computer by linking it to a bureau machine. It has been suggested that the capital outlay involved in such a system could be cut by using a modem instead of the office computer. The work that can be done without a computer, however, is limited so that with such an alternative arrangement, frequent access would have to be made to the central machine. This, plus the relatively high cost of program storage on bureau computers, would make the running costs of this type of set-up at least as expensive, while being by no means as convenient.

Once the architect has mastered the day-to-day use of such a system, he will be able to extend the field of programs that he employs, and with the aid of the computer become involved in aspects of design which he has previously avoided because of their mathematical content. With additional training and experience to back this involvement, the prospects for total design would be greatly improved.

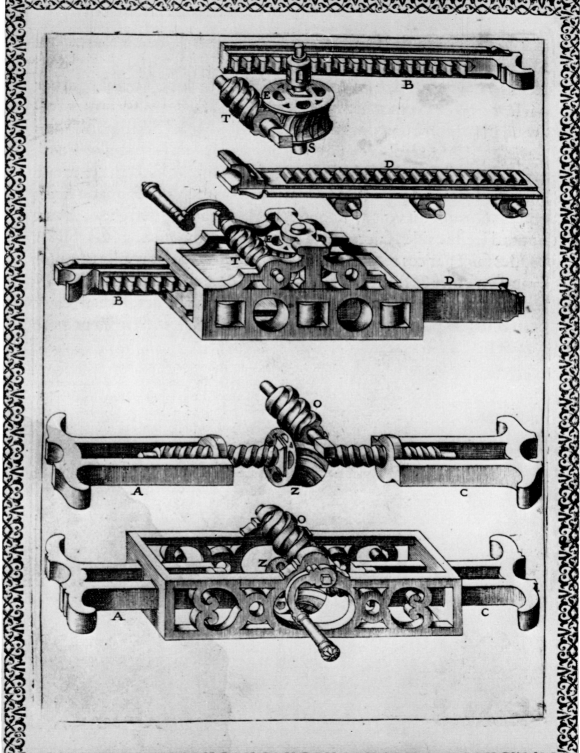

4 BASYS

4.1 Hardware and System

The BASYS System, which is being developed by a team at the Imperial College of Science and Technology, London, is an automated-draughting software package conceived in terms of the needs of building designers. That is to say architects, structural engineers, plant engineers and surveyors.

The package employs the hardware already described. A PDP-8/e computer with teletype, four DECtape Units, a CADMAC Table for digitising-plotting and a TEKTRONIX 611 Storage Tube monitor with a joystick pointer. The teletype has, of course, a paper tape reader and punch, and the table is fitted with a parallel motion straight edge to aid in the preparation of pre-digitising sketches.

The system also includes a pair of 5 digit numerical displays. Each display has a plus-minus sign and three alternative decimal point indicators, the latter being manually controlled. The numerical displays are not linked directly to read the coordinates of the gantry position on the table, but indirectly via the computer so that the digitiser position can be displayed to scale, or the actual movement corrected to controlled sizes or directions before being displayed and digitised.

In Photograph 36 the computer, magnetic tape unit and interfaces can be seen mounted in a single cabinet. This prototype machine uses only two DECtape Units and has an additional DECtape checking display mounted at the very top of the cabinet which is not part of the system when in use. The diagrammatic layout in Figure 37 shows the computer cabinet arranged in a horizontal format, suitable for wall hanging over a layout space arranged at the side of the table. The figure also

36
The hardware used to develop the BASYS System

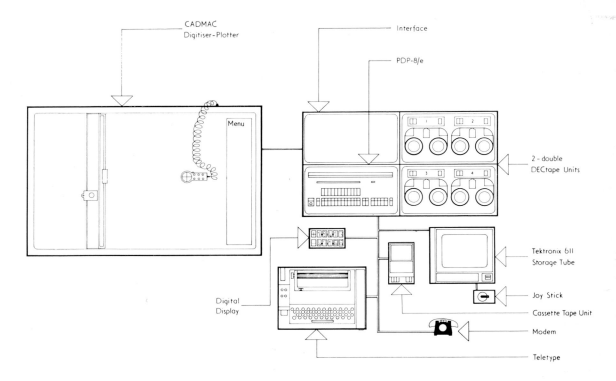

CADMAC
Digitiser-Plotter

Menu

Interface

PDP-8/e

2 - double
DECtape Units

Tektronix 611
Storage Tube

Joy Stick

Cassette Tape Unit

Modem

Teletype

Digital
Display

37
Diagrammatic layout of BASYS
System hardware

shows an additional item in the form of a cassette tape reader which it is proposed to include in the system.

When a position of the gantry is digitised, the value recorded is to an accuracy of 0·1 mm at a scale of 1 : 1 (i.e. full size). When a drawing is being prepared to a scale of, say, 1 : 100, this represents 1 cm. This means that objects cannot be drawn to dimensions which are fractions of a centimetre at this scale. This is no problem as in general drawings of this scale do not show details which require sub-divisions to milli-metres. When details are enlarged, the parts will be plotted to the larger scale as having sizes in round centimetres, and smaller details can be added without any problem.

When drawings are plotted to a smaller scale than digitised, the plotter always draws as close as possible to the digitised dimensions, rounding them up to the nearest 0·1 mm of actual drawn size—which is the limit of accuracy of the plotter. A drawing digitised to a scale of 1 : 1000 could only show objects to the nearest decimetre when plotted; however, such small-scale site layouts are not logically part of a working drawing system. It is assumed that the major sections would be at a scale of 1 : 50, 1 : 100 or 1 : 200, and details would be added at 1 : 5, 1 : 10 or 1 : 20. The scales normally available directly from the menu card range from 1 : 1000 to 1 : 1. The limitations involved in interrelating drawings of greatly differing scales are no greater than is found in normal practice, as objects on drawings can be digitised to an accuracy greater than it is possible to set the digitising head by use of a program called DIGIPLUS. This program allows extra digits to be specified on the teletype and added to the displayed figures before the value is stored. The use of DIGIPLUS as a means of digitising is very slow compared to the normal procedure, but it does allow the occasional use of, for example, a dimensioned survey drawing, parts of which are required to an enlarged scale for a series of interrelated site plans. In all cases, the values stored on the magnetic tape are the full-size dimensions of the object. The drawing produced by the plotter is to a scale specified by the operator, usually by reference to the menu card; thus, once digitised, a drawing or part of it can be reproduced to any scale within the limits of the size of the table.

4.2 Magnetic Tape Storage

All the operating programs for the PDP-8/e are stored on magnetic tape on the first reader, and can be called to the Core Store of the computer, either by the menu card on the table or by the teletype.

The second tape reader is used to store the major sections as they are digitised. The DECtape is divided into 1,474 addressable blocks, each of 129–12 bit words. Thus each block can be addressed as part of a major section, and information can be digitised on several different major sections and all stored together on the same tape. Each time a different major section is referred to, a new block must be started and addressed accordingly; however, when information is plotted, only that in blocks with the address of a given drawing will be plotted.

The address can also be varied in part in order to permit 'trial details' to be tested. If the result is unsatisfactory, the trial detail can be erased without affecting the basic drawing or the other details which are satisfactory. With such a breakdown of addresses, it is possible to store, for example, a basic grid of columns only once, and yet plot them on several floor plans. This arrangement also permits various 'levels' of drawing, so that such a grid plus a few other details can be plotted and supplied for use as layout drawings to those producing structural or service details.

The third tape reader is for tapes on which are stored standard details. Each standard detail is coded by its address, and may contain variables which are specified while the detail is displayed on the monitor. The detail with variables specified is transferred to the major section tape, addressed, then included as part of any, or all, of the major sections on that tape. Each detail has a fully coded address and can be cross-

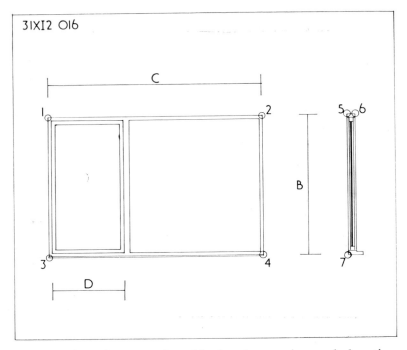

31X12 016

C

B

D

referenced, as for example, with the plan section and elevation of the same detail, and to other information (such as price or manufacturer's name) which can be listed on other tapes to be used on the fourth reader. Groups of details can often share parts. Thus a manufacturer's window range may use the same sill and head detail for many different sizes of window. The digitised values for the head or sill are stored only once, and the possible overall sizes stored separately. When the detail for a particular size of window is transferred to the major section tape, the various parts automatically are fitted together.

The fourth tape reader is required mostly for coding and billing purposes which will be described in greater detail in the next chapter. It is also used for copying from any of the other tapes and for updating master tapes.

Figure 37 also includes a cassette tape reader which can be used for small items which it may not be convenient to store on the standard detail tape. Such things as trees, vehicles and furniture outlines for example, and other items relating to each building type. The cassette tape can also be used as a cheap means by which manufacturers can supply standard details for their products to the designer. It also provides a contact between the designer and the computer system which is outside the formal set-up of the four DECtape handlers, and which can therefore be at a more personal even humorous level.

The information stored on the DECtapes is in groups of words, each group representing either a point on a drawing or a code. The codes have two basic forms, namely line codes or information codes. A line code directs the computer to read the words which follow it up to the next code word, and uses them to plot a particular type of line, or group of lines. The information code directs the computer to read a specified number of the words which follow it, and treat them as information to be used as directed by the code word and the program. Information codes have several uses, including Product Index Coding which defines the material or product represented by the line codes and lines which follow it. Product Index Codes are described in more detail in the next chapter.

The different types of code words are distinguished by varying combinations of the first three bits of the word, thus leaving nine bits for information. Line codes must be followed by the necessary number of pairs of double precision words (24 bits each) to give the data required to position the line or lines specified by the line code. A double precision word is sufficient to specify a single coordinate of a point on a drawing, so two are required to specify both x and y coordinates. To draw a single straight line the coordinates of both ends of it are required, which is four double precision words plus a single word for the line code.

When drawing a series of continuous straight lines, it is only necessary to specify each intersection once, as this will be treated as the end of one line and the beginning of the next. For circular arcs three points must be specified; the centre of the circle and each end of the arc, in a clockwise direction, in that order.

4.3 Digitising

Digitising is carried out on the top surface of the CADMAC Table, using a digitiser which consists of a magnified cross-hair with a press button mounted on one side. This can be used in either hand, but as the action is very simple the question of left- or right-handedness hardly arises.

The standard digitiser available with this system has a further set of eight function buttons mounted on one side, which are operated with the free hand. The use of these buttons can be introduced one at a time. Their purpose is to speed the digitising process by allowing operations normally referred to via the menu card to be called directly without moving the digitiser away from the work in hand.

An alternative arrangement has sixteen function buttons on a separate block independent of the digitiser. This larger number of buttons is useful if the operator wishes to write figures directly on the drawing, as this can be done from the block which is large enough to have all ten digits plus decimal points, etc. In general, however, other techniques are available for dimensioning for which the eight button standard digitiser is sufficient.

The techniques for digitising have been developed mostly in the fields of cartography and machine tool control. In both these cases, the object of digitising is to obtain from an accurate drawing the position of any points upon it which can be used for a particular purpose. With cartography, it is to plot a map which emphasizes different features to those predominant in the original. In the case of machine tool control, it is normally to plan the path of a cutter which will produce a copy in metal of the original drawing. Neither of these situations relate to the objectives of digitising in a design office, so it is hardly surprising that the techniques previously developed are of little use.

The object of digitising in a design office is to assemble data in order that a working drawing and schedule can be prepared accurately and quickly from an initial drawing which may be a far from accurate sketch. To the architect, the accuracy of a drawing is not very important, for in practice drawings are never scaled, but all sizes are determined either from the dimensions on the drawing or from the relative position of the object with a previously defined grid drawn over the entire drawing. Digitising for the designer, therefore, is more a matter of storing points at given dimensions than of attempting to accurately position a digitiser over a point on a drawing.

The basic programs of BASYS have been designed to facilitate this process and are described in the remainder of this section. All these programs make use of what is called a Trailing Origin. Each major section or detail has an origin usually just outside the bottom left-hand corner of the drawn details, from which the coordinates of all the digitised points are measured. This is the Base Origin of the drawing and is the normal origin from which the digital display reads. When using a trailing origin, however, each digitised point becomes the origin for the readout on the digital display. This does not affect the value actually stored, but simply means that the digital display shows each true coordinate of the digitiser minus the value of the coordinates, at the last previously digitised point.

GRID: With this program the user specifies a grid size and the readings on the digital display and the value store after digitising are those of the nearest grid intersection to the position of the digitising head. In order to be able to draw off the grid, the program also allows by use of the button controls on the head for the digital display to show trailing origin values which are not on the grid. Thus when, for example, an object is to be digitised which has one side on a grid, this side is digitised first, the trailing origin is then introduced and the other side set out relative to the first. The original sketch can be made on squared paper to match the grid used, and the off-grid dimensions indicated in figures.

60

The universal use of grids for planning has been predicted for many years, but for several reasons their use appears unlikely ever to become total. For work which is not on a grid therefore, an alternative program is provided.

CONTROL 15: This program provides a very similar control over the digitiser to that provided for the user by a draughting machine in normal drawing office practice. The trailing origin is used, and when the digitiser head is moved from a previously digitised point, the program assumes that it is the user's intention to move along a line which is at one of the fixed 15° angles (i.e. 0°, 15°, 30°, 45° . . . 180°) which are obtained on the click stop rotary head of a draughting machine. The digital readout, therefore, indicates on one axis the true movement, and on the other a computed value which corresponds to the trigonometrical relation between the first readout and the 15° angle which is nearest to the actual angle at which the digitiser has been moved. As the digitiser is moved about the board, the computer continues to make this correction at a speed which permits the values to be changed several times a second.

This may sound complicated but it is quite simple to understand in an example. Suppose the operator has digitised a point, and now wishes to digitise another point which is 200 mm away to the right in a horizontal line on the drawing. That is to say, using trailing origin, he is looking for the values $x = 0.2000$ and $y = 0.0000$. Once he has digitised the first point, the readouts will both read 0 until he moves the digitiser. Under normal circumstances, if the digitiser is then moved approximately 200 mm to the left, the x coordinate will read something like 0.1994 and the y 0.0008. The operator will then need to manipulate the head in two dimensions in order to get the value he wants. This is quite difficult and time-consuming, because any attempt to correct one value invariably changes the other.

With CONTROL 15, however, when the operator moves the digitiser approximately horizontally, only the x readout gives a true reading and the y readout reads zero. Obtaining the precise readout required on one axis is then quite easy. If the head is displayed slowly away from the horizontal line, the time will come when the digitiser is nearer an angle of 15° than it is to the horizontal, whereupon the y readout will give a value corresponding to the x readout which is the y coordinate for an angle of 15° ($y = x \tan 15°$). If the displacement is further increased, the y readout will change first to correspond to an angle of 30° and then 45°. For angles larger than 45°, the y readout shows the true displacement and the x readout is corrected to correspond with angles of 60°, 75° and 90°.

CONTROL 90 + A: This program provides the equivalent of that which is obtained when the head on a draughting

61

machine is locked at an angle A. The same type of correction is applied as in CONTROL 15 but only for two directions, one in a line at an angle A and the other perpendicular to it. This permits, for example, two buildings whose plans are at an acute angle to each other to be drawn on the same sheet.

The first is drawn square to the sheet using CONTROL 15, then CONTROL 90 + A is used to tilt the angle of the digitising process to the required angle for the second building and the second plan drawn. The facility of drawing at 15° intervals to the tilted axis is not provided for. Although an experienced draughtsman can easily distinguish by eye 15° intervals from the horizontal, he cannot be expected to do so from an axis which is tilted to an angle. Several values for angle A can be stored in the computer and called upon one at a time from the menu card, so a complex group of irregularly arranged plans can be digitised using this system without any difficulty.

FIND: This program is used to trace a previously digitised point in order to be able to erase or further extend the digitising from that point. This is done after calling the program FIND on the menu card by digitising the point as accurately as possible on the drawing, and then waiting for the program to search through the previously digitised points to find the one closest to that just digitised.

This process of locating a previously digitised point is not easy, for if CONTROL 15 has been used, the drawing may have been digitised to a greater accuracy than it was originally drawn. Problems can arise when, for example, it is proposed to extend a brick pier from a point immediately adjacent to a window. Care must be taken in picking up the edge of the pier not to get a point on the window frame instead. If, however, all the items previously digitised have been correctly product coded, this is not a problem as FIND can be instructed to distinguish between products and in this case only to search for a point listed as brick.

As each block of points is digitised, it should be checked by displaying it on the storage tube. This is not a check on the accuracy of the digitising, which can be checked as it is performed, as much as upon the digitising process.

Only a very cursory investigation is required into everyday drawing office practice to discover the fact that the vast majority of the construction lines on drawings are drawn parallel to one or other of the major axes of the drawing. It will also be found that most lines are also part of an enclosed rectilinear boundary which represents the outline of an object either sectioned or as seen in elevation.

A small group of programs have been included in the BASYS Package to speed the construction of this type of line of which the following two are the most used.

39
Illustration for RECTCON Program

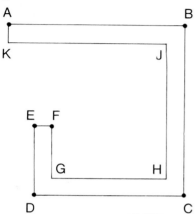

RECTANGLE: Using CONTROL 15, the bottom left corner of any complete rectangle required is digitised. The menu card position RECTANGLE is then digitised, and the digitiser positioned relative to the original bottom left corner, still under CONTROL 15 so as to give first a zero readout on the y axis digital display and the required x axis reading for the rectangle, then a zero readout on the x axis digital display and the other required y axis reading for the rectangle. Each of these positions is digitised and the values stored result in the construction upon plotting of the complete rectangle.

RECTCON: Using CONTROL 15, a linked series of straight lines are constructed after digitising RECTCON on the menu card, see ABCDE in Figure 39. The associated menu card position RECTGAP is then digitised, followed by a further point F on the drawing. The values stored will result in the construction, upon plotting of the complete ring ABCDEFGHJKA where FG, GH, HJ and JK are a linked series of straight lines, each of which is parallel to the corresponding part of the original digitised series A to E and at the distance EF from it.

4.4 Plotting
Plotting on the CADMAC Table is done on the lower surface beneath the gantry. The plotter head can contain either a ball-point pen or an Indian ink draughting pen. The latter draws a better quality line and would normally be used for all finished drawings, but the former is less liable to dry up and can be left for long periods without attention.

The CADMAC System controls the plotter head in two dimensions, and causes it to pass between each pair of digitised points in the mode specified by the line code. This can be a straight line, an arc of a circle or a conic section.

The Program CONIC-TANGENT permits a number of conic sections to be joined to produce complex flowing curves which can be made to approximate to a free curve, as can normally be done using a choice from a range of French curves. Each type of line can be further modified by the use of an interrupt on the pen control which results in a dotted line being drawn. When the plotter is in action, no contact with it is possible apart from stopping it, so the output is entirely dependent upon previously digitised material and specified standard details. It is possible, of course, to add to what appears by sketching a missing detail, digitising it and plotting it upon the drawing. Such a procedure should not occur, however, when final drawings are being prepared, for all the plotting required should then be available from all the major sections.

4.5 Assembling and Dimensioning
The form of the final list of working drawings and schedules prepared for a contract is entirely the choice of the system user.

It is to be expected, however, that if the BASYS System is used as proposed, the drawings produced will consist of a set of major sections labelled as 'Plans', 'Sections' and 'Elevations' in the traditional way plus a series of large-scale details from the major sections which can be assembled to provide trade, sub-contract and assembly drawings.

A logical pattern results from this system, whereby the enlarged details are all visible to a smaller scale on a major section. If for some reason, however, additional details are required which do not easily relate in this way, they can be drawn by hand or prepared by hand modification of other details which are available from the major sections.

The BASYS System is thus very flexible and permits almost any approach to the preparation of drawings to be integrated with it. On the other hand, if an office design policy exists or is planned, it is possible by means of this system to apply it throughout a large office to ensure that only tested and approved details are used on a specified grid, and presented to an agreed format.

BASYS is clearly well suited to the drawing up of building systems where a limited number of previously designed and digitised components can be called from the standard details tape and assembled rapidly into a design. The system builder has the added advantage that his component will be accurately costed both for manufacturing and assembling, so a simple schedule of parts will provide him with a priced bill of quantities, at least for the superstructure, within minutes of digitising the final layout drawings.

Architects normally choose to use a wider range of standard details than are available in a building system, and will also expect to use materials other than in component form. In such cases, it will still be necessary to have costings prepared, but all the advantages of time-saving and speed in the preparation of the working drawings and schedules are available plus the direct association of the designer with this preparation and the labour saving this produces. If the difference between the scale used to plot a major section drawing and that used to digitise details is not too great, then at the point when the final version of the major sections are used as plans, sections and elevations, all the information stored on the major section can be plotted. If, however, the major section is very large and some very complex details have been included, the quality of the final drawing may be impaired if too much detail is included. This can be overcome, as explained above, by coding each major section to different levels.

Normally all details can be included in a general plan section or elevation without detracting from the drawing, but when such drawings are required for special purposes such as service layouts it can help to exclude them.

64

Sheets of detail can be assembled by specifying parts of a major section and the point upon the paper on which it is to be drawn. This is a simple process which requires the operator to assemble a series of three instructions:

(1) the vertical and horizontal dimensions of a rectangle which would contain the details required from the major section,

(2) the coordinates relative to the base origin of the major section of the bottom left-hand corner of the rectangle,

(3) the coordinates relative to the base origin of the detail sheet at which this same corner must be placed for the details to be plotted in the required position on the detail sheet.

As long as the scale setting is correct and there is sufficient space on the paper for the details, then plotting should proceed as required without interaction by the operator. The same use can be made of level codes in this type of plotting, as in the plotting of major sections to eliminate any part of the detail not required for the purpose of the particular drawing.

The dimensioning of a drawing in traditional practice is frequently a somewhat haphazard business. The procedure normally employed is as follows. A dimension line is drawn parallel to the space or object to be dimensioned, indicator lines are drawn perpendicular to the dimension line to stop just short of the points to which the dimension must refer, and then figures are placed against the dimension line indicating the distance between the indicator lines. Sufficient dimensions are added until it is felt that the sizes and/or positions of all the objects shown are fully specified.

The system program DIMENSION is designed to follow a similar procedure but with a somewhat improved logic. The program can be used directly upon a drawing which has been plotted; alternatively a sheet of tracing paper can be placed over the drawing, and the dimension prepared on the top sheet, stored on a magnetic tape on the fourth reader and then re-plotted on the drawing by reading back from the tape after the top sheet has been removed.

The dimension lines and indicator lines required are decided, and then sketched by hand on the drawing or the cover sheet, which is then placed on the digitising surface and digitised using the program DIMENSION which requires only one point per indicator line and one more point per dimension line to be digitised for the full pattern of the dimensioning group, i.e. dimension line, dotted indicator lines and intersection crosses or arrowheads to be stored. The figures for each dimension are also plotted at this point. With the aid of DIMENSION this can be done by either of two basically different techniques.

The first involves using FIND to trace the exact position of the points being dimensioned. With DIMENSION–FIND, a readout is obtained on one of the digital displays as to the

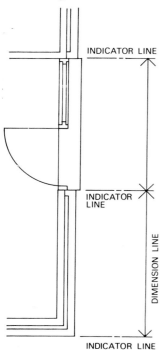

40
Illustration for DIMEN-SION Program

INDICATOR LINE

INDICATOR LINE

DIMENSION LINE

INDICATOR LINE

DIGITISE

To digitise a line each appropriate space on the card must be digitised beginning with '*start*' followed by the shape required and the type of line (i.e. continuous, dotted, etc.). Before digitising, a file should be opened to receive the drawing data or macro detail. If no file is opened, the data will be retained in the computer buffer from which it can be displayed but not stored.

FILE

Two storage buffers are available, one for drawing data, the other for macros. By digitising the appropriate location on the card the option to open an appropriate file is obtained and the file is chosen by naming it on the teletype. The contents of the buffer are transferred to the file either when the buffer is full (thus clearing it to be refilled) or when one of the *close file* spaces is digitised.

LETTERING

To include alph-numeric characters in a file digitise *call*, specify size required on teletype, and digitise choice from four styles. Script is then typed and position of first character digitised on drawing.

MACROS

To display a macro on the storage tube digitise *call* and specify file number on teletype. File number for a macro is a C1/SfB/P1 code of either a product or a component. To set dimensions, digitise *fix* and specify each dimension A, B, C, etc., on the teletype, use *hand*, $+A°$, $+90°$, or $-90°$, to orientate macro specifying A° on teletype if required. Digitise *point* followed by choice of corner of macro 1, 2, 3, etc. Digitise *to data* followed by a position on the major section, the position being that of the chosen corner. Each time *to data* is digitised the same macro can be again positioned at a new location.

ERASE

To erase the last line digitise *last line*. To erase the entire buffer digitise *buffer*, then type Y after the query *IS BUFFER TO BE ERASED?* appears on the teletype print-out.

DISPLAY AND PLOT

Digitising *data buffer*, *macro buffer* or *current file* causes the contents to be displayed on the storage tube. Likewise for *a file*, but in this case the file name must also be typed. The same also applies to the plotting routines, but in each case the appropriate location on the plotting area, and the scale, must be specified.

SLIDERULE

The menu card section SLIDERULE provides the means of carrying out the four basic arithmetical operations to the contents of the two digital registers. This can be done to figures already present in the registers or by use of *clear* followed by the digits *0* to *9*, both registers can be filled with the required values. When an arithmetical operation is performed the result appears in the X register and the Y is left clear. Further use of the digits fills only the Y register, after which a further operation can be performed, and so on.

With this menu card the program CONTROL 15 is available once *start* is digitised. It is brought into operation by one of the function buttons on the digitiser head. The menu card location *to data* is also available through a function button.

BASYS 1

DIGITISE		
start	line	
arc	circle	
———	--------	
– – –	–·–·–	

FILE		
open data file	close data file
open macro file	close macro file

LETTERING		
call	size
style A	style B
style C	style D

MACROS		
call	fix
hand	$+A°$
$+90°$	$-90°$
point	to data

ERASE		
last line	a line
buffer	

DISPLAY		
data buffer	macro buffer
current file	a file

PLOT		
data buffer	macro buffer
current file	a file

SLIDERULE			
1	2	3	+
4	5	6	−
7	8	9	×
O	clear	÷

on
off

1971
© BASYS LTD

41
MENU CARD No. 1

distance, i.e. horizontal or vertical between two adjacent points, and the value obtained can be transferred directly to the dimension line at a point specified by the digitiser. For diagonal dimensions, the readout is always on the storage tube but otherwise the same procedure applies.

The use of FIND on many points on a large drawing can, however, be very slow, and especially with a regular layout where the experienced designer has most of the dimensions in his head and can find the remainder quickly, it is quite feasible to return to traditional practice and add the dimension from the known figures. In this case, the dimension can be registered in the display for transfer to the tape by use of either the block of function buttons mentioned above, or by the teletype, or by digitising digits from a numbered grid on the menu card.

This last-mentioned grid is that shown on the bottom of the menu card in Figure 41 which is part of the program SLIDE RULE which permits simple arithmetical calculations, similar to that available on a slide rule, plus addition and subtraction, to be carried out using this grid on the menu card as a calculation machine keyboard and the digital display as a pair of registers. The process of dimensioning is improved by the use of the subprogram DIMENSION–CHECK. This program depends on the fact that a logically dimensioned drawing has a set of dimensions which should provide a grid which intersects all the digitised points of the drawing—at least at a certain level on that drawing. If this level can be identified in the hierarchy of the addressing system, then DIMENSION–CHECK can be set to compare the dimensions coded and the drawing at that level, and will print out on the teletype any discrepancies between the two. It is thus a check for both inaccurate dimensions and for the existence of undimensioned points.

The type of dimensioning and the amount required is totally dependent upon the user's design. By the use of a grid or a dimension pattern, an automatic dimensioning technique could be devised which would greatly speed the preparation of the finished drawings. The BASYS System does not, however, impose the use of any such techniques and the standard program provides the maximum aid possible to traditional dimensioning methods.

4.6 Notes, Titles and Finishes

A full range of sizes of alpha-numeric characters are available with the BASYS System, so titles can be added by positioning the plotter head and typing the letters required on the teletype. Typing can be first displayed on the storage tube, checked and then plotted on the drawing. Position checking of small amounts of lettering can be done by first plotting on an overlay.

Standard titles, headings and blocks of notes can be stored on cassette tapes and repeated on each drawing, as can the logo type-face of a commercial client, which can be digitised from a photographic blow-up and then reproduced to any scale. The work involved in reconstructing a complex symbol can, however, be considerable and such embellishments if required are best photographically reproduced on transparent stickers.

The program HATCH is used to cross-hatch, shade or draw brick and block courses upon specified areas. The program draws horizontal, vertical or forty-five degree diagonal lines at specified spaces within the boundary of any digitised space. It can be specified by a code number when digitising. The code follows immediately after the product code, and specifies the type of hatching which is to be carried out on the digitised area which follows, if the program HATCH is in operation at the time of plotting.

Alternatively, the hatching can be added later by specifying in the sub-program data that the digitised areas within certain product codes must be hatched in a certain way. The hatching code has a similar hierarchical structure to that of the DECtape code, so that if required certain areas can be cross-hatched when plotting and others, although previously coded, left plain.

It is clearly desirable to plot each drawing to a finished state, and there is no reason why this should not be done. It is none the less quite acceptable for the user to hand-finish a drawing by adding to the plotting where he feels that this will improve its value. In particular, the use of a heavier line to emphasize part of a piece of construction may improve legibility. Elevations are often enhanced by the addition of shadows, and although this can be achieved by hatching areas with a plotter, it may be more effective to handle them in a less formal way. The use of transparent stickers has already been mentioned, and is more logical than an attempt to digitise very complex shapes.

4.7 Multiple User Application

The BASYS System, as described to date, is used by a single operator with a PDP-8/e and 8K Core Store and a CADMAC Table. The PDP-8/e can have Core Storage of up to 32K, and time-sharing programs exist that permit one machine to be used by up to four digitisers simultaneously.

A system is now being developed which provides for the simultaneous working of four users while digitising, and one plotter which is outputting. Such a system can be used by four operators, each of whom must have a digitiser, a DECtape reader for his major section tape, and possibly a second for coding. Additional shared tapes are required for standard details and the programs. The plotter, if not in use as a digitiser, can plot simultaneously while the others are digitising. It is also planned to arrange for the sequential plotting of drawings on an automatically transported roll of paper. As long as only ball-point plotting is required, this can be done unattended.

68

The economics and convenience of such a system are yet to be tested, but it could prove a much cheaper way of introducing the system to a larger office than would be possible with the original proposal. It should, of course, be quite possible to extend a one-man system to a multiple system simply by the addition of extra equipment and Core Stores.

4.8 The 8K FORTRAN Package

The user of the BASYS System has to hand a PDP-8/e computer with all the program packages which have been developed by both the manufacturer and DECUS, a users' society which has a library available to members of over seven hundred programs. Probably most significant of all these programs is the 8K FORTRAN package.

FORTRAN is a high-level language developed by IBM, and is especially suited to the type of calculation associated with architectural and engineering problem solving. The BAID Programs described in the next chapter are written in FORTRAN.

To use programs written in this language is quite simple, although the limited size of the machine available must be kept in mind. The real value of possessing this package is, however, the opportunity it offers for writing programs. The FORTRAN language uses conventional mathematical symbols and English language words and a training course in its use takes about one week. Although the size of program which can be operated effectively on the 8K PDP-8/e is limited, practically all large programs are written as an assembly of sub-programs. It is thus possible to debug and test the sub-programs separately, then assemble the full program for use on a larger machine, possibly via the modem.

The increasing popularity of these small machines has focussed attention upon techniques for running larger programs than would previously have been thought practical. The basic approach is to use a large computer to prepare a very efficiently operating small main program, which calls a large number of small sub-programs, only one of which is required at any given time. In this way the core storage required for the program is kept to a minimum. Such programs are, of course, very slow and the intention is that they should be run outside office hours. Thus an architect using a draughting system of the type described could exchange his system tapes for program and data tapes before leaving the office in the evening, and set the program to operate during the night. A program which would run in say fifteen minutes on a large bureau machine might take all night on the small office machine, but the outlay would be considerably reduced.

5

BASYS APPLICATIONS

5.1 Coding Systems

It is standard practice for design engineers in industry to prepare assembly drawings for their designs, on which each item is coded and referred to a separate shop drawing upon which are given full production details for this particular item. This procedure is also used by the architect when extensive prefabrication is undertaken, but until now, he has not considered the return obtained from numbering every item on his drawings to be worth the effort and time involved.

Some items which are traditionally made off-site, such as doors and windows, are scheduled and this normally involves numbering each item on the drawings. However, if an attempt is made to code all the parts of a traditionally constructed building, problems arise in deciding the degree of sub-division to be employed. Clearly one should not number each individual brick, but one might expect to number every beam. It can happen that a building contains hundreds of identical beams, and no purpose is served by giving each a separate code number. This repetition of many identical items within a whole which in its totality is unique is a particular characteristic of building; most industries assemble products consisting of many different parts, with little repetition, but the final products are intended to be identical. Not surprisingly, therefore, the architect requires a different coding system to that used by engineering designers, one which possesses a flexibility in the depth of its subdivisions ranging from a loose classification of parts to a detailed codification of the smallest detail.

In developing a coding system, it is first necessary to decide the level at which the coding is required in order to distinguish between dissimilar items. This level is largely a matter of degree of fabrication. If it were common practice to change the type of door handle from one door to another throughout a building, then it would be desirable to code the various types of door handles. In practice, however, most doors of a given type will have the same handle throughout a project, so it is usually more simple to code the doors complete with ironmongery and classify a change of handle as a different door.

With such items as bricks and blocks, each type listed by the manufacturer and used on a project would require to be coded, while on the drawing this code would be used to specify each wall, not of course each brick. Similarly, in the case of other products which are used in bulk such as floor finishes, ceiling tiles, and paints, etc., the product code would relate to areas on a drawing and to the code used by the manufacturer.

The number of codes required is clearly going to be quite large. It has been estimated that there are over a million products in the building industry, and most large projects will contain several thousand different items. The risk of recognition error and the difficulty of tracing a particular product through a simple code number suggests that the products should first be classified. The purpose of such a classification, besides assisting with recognition, is to aid in grouping the products to be used: first, for comparison to allow the most suitable to be selected, and second, to assist in collecting together like-products for scheduling. In addition to classification, each product will require a code number within its group but such a code will be quite small. Ideally, the classification system should be designed as part of both the product selection index and the scheduling method, but in practice classification systems are usually planned for ease of product selection and are adopted for scheduling purposes afterwards. This must be due in part to the fact that product selection is a clearly defined process, whereas with detailed scheduling as is required in the preparation of Bills of Quantity, several alternative relationships can be emphasized in listing the same materials and labour. Such schedules are commonly made in terms of a classification of the building craft carrying out the work, or in terms of the activities and operations required to be performed in the process of building or in terms of a classification of products.

The first of these is the traditional form in which Bills of Quantity are prepared in England, and is known as a Trade Bill. The Trade Bill is basically designed for pricing purposes. It has little value on site as an aid to building, and tends to support the concept of inviolable craft boundaries into which every innovation must be inserted.

The second, or Operations Bill, appears at first to be the most logical but it does imply that the entire building operation is preplanned at the design stage—which must in many cases mean before the contractor has been appointed. It is claimed by those who champion this form of Bill that a means should be found to appoint a contractor at a very early stage, but it is questionable whether, in the majority of cases, the best interest of the client is served by so doing. If a situation developed where the architect's office took over the planning and organization of the building contract, and the contractor tendered only for the supply of materials and labour, then the Operations Bill approach would be the obvious and logical means of scheduling, both for site organization and tendering. There are those who consider this to be the future pattern for the industry, but while the present method of tendering and site organization continues, the Elemental Bill, which groups together like-materials and the labour associated with them, will probably be the best all-round technique for scheduling.

The third type, the Elemental Bill, although not as useful on site as the Operations Bill, provides schedules of materials for stock checking and allows the labour and specification clauses associated with each to be easily cross-referenced. The classification required is also that of a product selection index.

72

5.2 CI/SfB Classification and PI Code

The SfB System first developed by the Swedish architect Lars Magnus Giertz is now internationally recognized for building materials' classification. The CI/SfB System is a British method of data coordination which is based, as its name implies, on the Swedish system. The CI/SfB method in essence is intended to provide data coordination for every item and process in building, so that all parts of each drawing and schedule can be completely cross-referenced, and all information relating to a particular building operation can be located rapidly by the man required to direct the work on site.[7]

It should be remembered that the ultimate objective of such a method must always be the provision of information to the site. This is not to decry the assistance such coordination can provide in the office, but if the true objective is lost sight of, and the use of such a system is assessed against traditional practice, the extra work involved in operating it can easily be considered unjustified. The CI/SfB Project Manual, published by the Royal Institute of British Architects, described the wider use of the method to classify drawings, schedules and even letters. Its primary use, however, is to classify building products for use on drawings and schedules, and it is this aspect which concerns us with BASYS.

The BASYS CI/SfB/PI is a product coding system, the classification part of which is based on CI/SfB. The classification is built up from three tables. Table 1 classifies building elements (i.e. floors, stairs, lighting, etc.). Table 2 classifies construction forms (i.e. excavation, pipes, flexible sheets, etc.). Table 3 classifies materials (i.e. wood, glass, cement, etc.). The classification appears sometimes to be rather broad but this is normally to avoid ambiguity.

The first Table contains sixty-four classifications of elements and is represented by a two-digit number in brackets. The second Table contains seventeen different construction forms, each of which is represented by a letter of the alphabet. The third Table contains twenty different materials groups, and again each is represented by a letter of the alphabet. Normally this last is a lower case letter, but in computer print-outs, such letters are rarely available and capitals are therefore used for both. There is, however, no risk of confusion because it is a cardinal rule of this system that Table 3 cannot be put into operation unless preceded by a value from Table 2, and neither can be used unless preceded by both digits of Table 1. The classifications from Table 1 can be used alone if required, and the materials in Table 3 can be further subdivided by the addition of a further digit.

The result is a classification of the type [27]Gi2 which specifies roof–truss–timber–softwood. To store this combination of digits and letters the 'American Standard Code for

Substructure	Superstructure			Services		Fittings	
(1–) Substructure	(2–) Primary elements	(3–) Secondary elements	(4–) Finishes	(5–) Services	(6–) Installations	(7–) Fixtures	(8–) Loose equipment
(10) Site substructure	(20) Site primary elements	(30) Site secondary elements	(40) Site finishes	(50) Site services	(60) Site installations	(70) Site fixtures	(80) Site loose equipment
(11) Excavations	(21) External walls	(31) External openings	(41) External finishes	(51) Refuse disposal	(61) Electrical source	(71) Circulation fixtures	(81) Circulation loose equipment
	(22) Internal walls	(32) Internal openings	(42) Internal finishes	(52) Drainage	(62) Power	(72) General room fixtures	(82) General room loose equipment
(13) Floorbeds	(23) Floors	(33) Floor secondary element	(43) Floor finishes	(53) Water supply	(63) Lighting	(73) Culinary fixtures	(83) Culinary loose equipment
	(24) Stairs	(34) Balustrades to stairs	(44) Stair finishes	(54) Gas	(64) Communications	(74) Sanitary fixtures	(84) Sanitary loose equipment
		(35) Suspended ceilings	(45) Ceiling finishes	(55) Refrigeration		(75) Cleaning fixtures	(85) Cleaning loose equipment
(16) Foundations				(56) Space heating	(66) Lifts transport	(76) Storage fixtures	(86) Storage loose equipment
(17) Piles	(27) Roofs	(37) Rooflights	(47) Roof finishes	(57) Ventilation			
	(28) Frames				(68) Security		

42
CI/SfB Table 1. Elements

Table 2		Table 3	
D	Formless materials	b	Aids, temporary works, plant
E	Cast in situ	c	Labour
F	Brick, block	d	Operations
G	Structural unit	e	Natural stone
H	Section, bar	f	Formed concrete, etc
I	Tube, pipe	g	Clay
J	Wire, mesh	h	Metal
K	Quilt	i	Wood
L	Foil, paper (except finishing paper)	j	Natural fibre
		m	Mineral fibre
M	Foldable sheet	n	Plastics, etc
N	Overlap sheet, tile	o	Glass
P	Thick coating	p	Loose fill
R	Rigid sheet	q	Cement, concrete
S	Rigid tile	r	Gypsum, etc
T	Flexible sheet, tile	s	Bituminous material
V	Thin coating including paint	t	Fixing, jointing agents
X	Components	v	Painting material
		w	Other chemicals
		x	Plants

43
CI/SfB Tables 2 and 3. Construction forms and materials

Information Interchange' (ASCII) is used which requires six bits per character, or thirty bits per CI/SfB classification. The BASYS System economizes somewhat on this by using ASCII for the letters and final digit, while reading the first two digits as octal numbers directly from the first six available bits of three words into which, as a result of this economy, the full CI/SfB number can be fitted.

To do this a special octal version of Table 1 has been devised. This involves two number changes (28) to (25) and (68) to (65) plus the use of (0–) instead of (8–). Both (25) and (65) are, of course, previously redundant spaces. A group of words representing a classification must, like any other information code, have machine recognition codes of three bits at the beginning of each word (see 4.2). Thus three words provide twenty-seven usable bits, while three ASCII characters and two octal numbers require twenty-four bits. The full CI/SfB/PI code is completed by a fourth word which contains the Product Index.

The Product Index (PI) is simply a numbered list of the different products in a given CI/SfB classification. The Index can be set up in whatever form suits the user. It can code the products on a particular project, or those used by an entire office. The nine bits permit just over five hundred different products to be coded per classification. Thus when the Product Index is set to zero the information code is a CI/SfB classifi-

44
Revised octal version of CI/SfB Table 1

Project

Substructure	Superstructure			Services		Fittings	
(1–) Substructure	(2–) Primary elements	(3–) Secondary elements	(4–) Finishes	(5–) Services	(6–) Installations	(7–) Fixtures	(0–) Loose equipment
(10) Site substructure	(20) Site primary elements	(30) Site secondary elements	(40) Site finishes	(50) Site services	(60) Site installations	(70) Site fixtures	(00) Site loose equipment
(11) Excavations	(21) External walls	(31) External openings	(41) External finishes	(51) Refuse disposal	(61) Electrical source	(71) Circulation fixtures	(01) Circulation loose equipment
	(22) Internal walls	(32) Internal openings	(42) Internal finishes	(52) Drainage	(62) Power	(72) General room fixtures	(02) General room loose equipment
(13) Floorbeds	(23) Floors	(33) Floor secondary element	(43) Floor finishes	(53) Water supply	(63) Lighting	(73) Culinary fixtures	(03) Culinary loose equipment
	(24) Stairs	(34) Balustrades to stairs	(44) Stair finishes	(54) Gas	(64) Communications	(74) Sanitary fixtures	(04) Sanitary loose equipment
	(25) Frames	(35) Suspended ceilings	(45) Ceiling finishes	(55) Refrigeration	(65) Security	(75) Cleaning fixtures	(05) Cleaning loose equipment
(16) Foundations				(56) Space heating	(66) Lifts transport	(76) Storage fixtures	(06) Storage loose equipment
(17) Piles	(27) Roofs	(37) Rooflights	(47) Roof finishes	(57) Ventilation			

cation, and when the Product Index is used it becomes a CI/SfB/PI Code. In special cases the unused three bits at the end of the third CI/SfB word can be combined with the PI word to extend the Product Index up to four thousand products per classification. It should be possible to code a library of products using this system, but for practical purposes there appears little benefit in spending time classifying a product in the BASYS System before it is to be used.

At present, in Britain, it is standard practice for each architect's office to collect a vast library of technical literature and spend many hours of tedious effort maintaining it. It appears likely that this practice will soon be superseded by the use of a national products file which will describe briefly most, if not all, of the products available—with advice on their use.[8] The designer will thus be able to select likely products, collect up-to-date information from the manufacturer, and so assemble a small products file for each project which will be thrown away at the end of the job.

Several different ways suggest themselves by which detailed information about a selected product could be transferred to an office system. For example, if each manufacturer possessed a modem, the required data could be requested by telephone and transferred automatically as a pretaped message from the manufacturer's office to the office computer. Alternatively, it may be cheaper for the manufacturer to post a cassette tape which could be read into the system and then returned or thrown away.

5.3 Product Codes and Schedules
The BASYS Program PRODCODE operates using a code tape on the fourth tape reader. The Program PRODCODE provides a means of accessing the product code word on the tape, either to modify it or for purposes of sorting. The PRODCODE Tape lists all the products coded by the user, and describes each both by the CI/SfB/PI code and by a brief description of the product sufficient for recognition in a schedule. This tape is prepared by the user, who adds each new product which he selects as he goes along. The method of working is decided upon by the user, but the following is a possible approach.

The user who is planning to set up a major section begins by preparing a rough list of the items likely to appear. This can be a list of actual product codes, but at this stage is more likely to be just CI/SfB classifications. This list is then typed on the teletype. The major section is digitised, and when a classification is required, the space PRODCALL on the menu card is digitised. This results in the typed list appearing on the storage tube, which will include either the brief product description, in the case of a full CI/SfB/PI code, or the recommended English language description in the case of

CI/SfB. The required code or classification is then selected by the joystick operated light spot and transferred to the major section tape as a product code by digitising the space CI/SfB/ PI on the menu card. The list shown on the storage tube can be extended at any time up to a total of fifty codes.

At a later date, as the major section becomes finalized, the need will arise to complete each product code where, previously, only a classification had been included. This is achieved by using PRODCODE. The required classification or, for that matter, any code which is to be changed, is listed on the tele-type, and the major section tape searched automatically for the listed numbers. Each time a number is found, it will be printed out on the teletype and the new value typed in. To check, a part of the tape can be shown on the storage tube before each new value is inserted. Each standard detail on the third tape will, of course, already be classified.

The BASYS Program SCHEDULE is used to list the product codes which appear on a major section and count the number of times each occurs. This is not a fully automatic way of scheduling, as the user must choose which major sections are to be worked upon and must guide the program to collect information logically. The appropriate major sections are normally the plans, each of which should show all the products which are on a given floor—partitions, doors, windows, fittings, etc.—as well as the area of the floor, the disposition of slabs, beams and columns, and areas of brick and block work.

The program copies all the product codes from each tape, and then tabulates them in elemental form based on the Tables of the CI/SfB classification. At this stage, the only quantities obtained are the totals for each item which has a product code. Certain items are listed as materials and not as products. A material item such as a brick wall or a water pipe has a product index describing the brick or pipe used but, as noted above, the program recognizes that the occurrence of the index code is not indicative of the use of a single product and lists those items separately and stores the addresses of the points on the major section tape at which they occur. The user must then plot the items listed and measure the quantities involved.

This measuring is done by hand in the case of pipes and wire runs, or by digitising and computation of areas and volumes in the case of materials such as floor tiles and brickwork. The standard details are, of course, all pre-measured and so this stage only applies to non-standard parts of the building.

The print-out is on teletype, and is subdivided into A4 paper sizes so that the roll can be cut into sheets and bound as a schedule or bill.

The BASYS Program DRAWCODE is used to write the classification or product code and English Language Description of any chosen item on a drawing which has already been plotted. The system is set as if to replot the drawing on top of the existing drawing. The plotter head traces each item, but with the pen raised so as not to mark the paper. As the head carries out the motion of drawing an item, the classification or product code of the item appears on the storage tube. At any moment during the motion, the user can stop the head, move it to a suitable position, and cause the pen to write the classification and English Language Description of the item it was in the process of tracing. When the writing is complete, the head will proceed to trace the next item. The movement of the head and the action of writing is controlled by the operator using the digitiser and function buttons.

5.4 Structural Design

The preparation of a structural design falls roughly into three phases. The first is the analysis of the structural shape, in which reference to the materials and member sizes to be used are needed only to determine the loading and stiffness of the members. The second is the checking of the member sizes. The third is the presentation of the results of the second in a form that can be interpreted by the fabricators and builders.

There have been two distinct approaches to the application of computers to the first of these phases, depending upon the magnitude of the structure involved. For large or complex structures, that is to say, structures which cover long spans, are of great height or complex form, the use of computers has led to the improvement of quality of these designs by permitting more subtle forms of analysis to be carried out than would otherwise be possible. The author's Gyrotron Structures referred to in the next chapter were analysed very closely by a method which it was estimated would have required 30,000 man-life-times of human calculation—had it been attempted without a computer.

A different approach has been applied to simple structures. By simple structures is meant a structure in which member sizes and spans are of traditional building dimensions, and the degree of interaction of the members is small. The building involved may be very large, but if the floor span and floor height are less than about 10 or 12 m, then the techniques for analysis will be well tried and to some degree standardized. The computer-aided design approach to this type of structure has been to merge the first two design stages by producing a program which will simultaneously analyse the structure and propose suitable member sizes. Smaller programs are also available which will design individual slabs, beams or columns in a similar way. The large majority of building structures fall into the class of simple structures, and this type of program provides the opportunity for the architect to obtain sizes for various alternative structural arrangements directly from a computer at the sketch design stage.

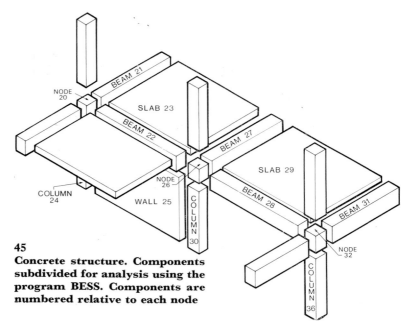

45
**Concrete structure. Components
subdivided for analysis using the
program BESS. Components are
numbered relative to each node**

The programs required to design entire structures in this way
are too large to be used on the PDP-8/e but can be accessed at a
bureau by means of the modem. An example of this type of
program is BESS (Building Engineering Sizing System), at
present being developed at the University of Leicester by
Mr. Andrew Main.[9] This program has a data structure by
which a slab and column, or slab, beam and column structure
can be defined, and a series of sub-programs which will carry
out stress analysis and member sizing automatically or under
guidance.

The present program assumes that wind-loading is carried by
sheer walls (i.e. staircase walls and lift shafts), as it is likely that
the program would be used initially for only relatively small
structures. There appear, however, to be no serious problems
preventing the program from being extended to allow for
wind-loading, thermal movement, earthquake-loading or any
other calculable design parameter.

The BESS user first defines his structure in terms of member
disposition, and then divides it into 'structural components',
i.e. slabs, beams and columns as shown in Figure 45. The
statutory loading, materials weights and slab construction is
then specified along with certain design preferences. These preferences include a choice of materials—reinforced concrete,
structural steel or composite, and in the case of reinforced
concrete the use of beams or beam strips. The latter, of course,
provide a slab with a beamless flat soffit. Although in the
diagrammatic subdivision in the figure the beams are shown as
rectangular, they are, in fact, designed as T or L beams where

applicable, and the reinforcement specified includes that required to make the floor slabs continuous over the beams.

When the structure has been so defined, it can be prepared on punched cards or tape and fed to the computer. The program then analyses the frame and chooses member sizes, and will then either print the results on a line printer or plot a section of the structure, marking on the member sizes.

GENESYS, the General Engineering System, is a government-backed and nationally maintained project to provide all civil and structural engineers in Britain with a comprehensive computer service.[10] It is organized by the Genesys Centre at the University of Loughborough, Leicestershire, England, who take full responsibility for the operation of the programs provided. The system is machine-independent and to date has programs for bridge and frame analysis and reinforced concrete design.

The purpose of this system is to provide an efficient method for solving engineering design problems by the use of a programming language and its compiler which is orientated specifically to structural design. The language in this case is called GENTRAN and is a version of FORTRAN. All users can write their own programs in this new language, and then allow their work to be marketed for them by the Genesys Centre.

The system already includes a number of major programs or sub-systems, two of which relate directly to building. FRAME-ANALYSIS/1 is used for the elastic analysis of two-dimensional frames or space frames.

A sub-system R.C. BUILD works in a similar way to BESS but more comprehensively, using an advanced structural analysis of the type preferred by more analytically minded engineers. GENESYS-R.C. BUILD is applicable to all sizes of concrete structure, and thus smaller programs like BESS may prove more appropriate for the type of building structure which it is envisaged an architect might design using a computer aid.

ICES, the Integrated Civil Engineering System, is a similar project, developed at the Massachusetts Institute of Technology, Cambridge, Mass., with a similar range of sub-systems and a FORTRAN based language called ICETRAN. This system is internationally available through IBM. The principal sub-system STRUDL-2 is a frame analysis program of a very advanced form, and is available on the IBM 360/65 machines. An earlier more simple version of this sub-system called STRESS is also available on the smaller IBM 1130.

5.5 Structural Detailing
The BASYS Program STEEL DETAILS is designed to assist the user in preparing layouts of steelwork for building or similar structures using rolled steel sections.

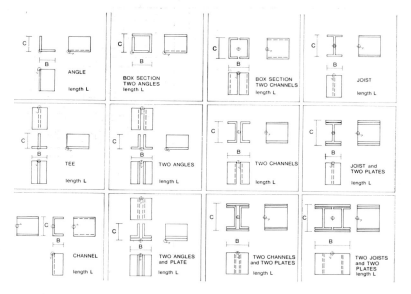

46
Macros used for preparation of structural steel layouts and detail by BASYS System

To prepare a floor plan, for example, the user chooses a section he wishes to use for a stanchion from the menu card (Figure 46), and specifies the dimensions B, C and the angle A degrees on the teletype. He digitises the positions in which he wants the stanchions centred, then adds the beams by choosing a section plan view from a menu card (specifying the dimensions B and L on the teletype), digitising in pairs the stanchions between which the beam is to span. The beam will then be fully digitised and, when plotted, will be drawn in between the two stanchions. A similar process is followed for sections and elevations, and in a similar way the side view of a section can be used to digitise both the longitudinal and diagonal members of a truss.

The drawing can be dimensioned using the program DIMENSION described earlier, and the member sizes noted beside the drawn shape or else coded and a schedule drawn up on one side of the drawing. Each member, as it is digitised, is coded with the SfB classification and provided with a PI number. Information stored on the scheduling tape on the fourth tape reader codes the description of the member in a standard format from which schedules can be prepared automatically which specify the number and length of each member and the total weight of each section used.

An extension of this program is planned which will allow the specification of rectangular hollow sections, a range of cold rolled sections, standard gusset, cleat details, and rivet, bolt and weld sizes, all from the menu card.

Very little has been done in Britain to standardize steel details, and this may account for the correspondingly small amount of work in this field by those interested in computer

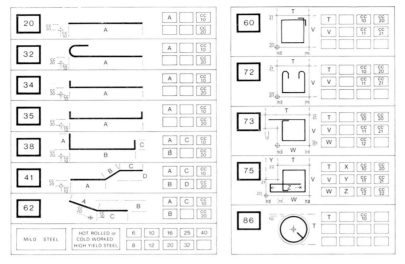

47
Macros used for preparation of reinforced concrete details by BASYS System

aids. The reverse is true of reinforced concrete detailing, which has been very closely standardized, and a number of computer-aided detailing systems have appeared. These systems have mostly been planned around computer terminals, and depend upon line printer outputs of standard beam and column sections which are not to scale, combined with bar schedules.

Grave doubts have been expressed about the use of standard sections which do not resemble either in proportion or scale the members they are supposed to represent. It may be found that errors do not occur as a result of this practice, or it may be that such systems will be superseded by methods which permit scale drawings to be prepared.

The BASYS Program CONCRETE DETAILS is such a program. A menu card provides a range of standard bar shapes specified in BS4466, and a selection of alternative beam and column sections, all of which have variable dimensions which can be specified on the teletype. When special bar shapes and member sections are required, they can be digitised fully using the normal digitising technique, but the standard items listed on the menu card will cover the large majority of cases. The methods of detailing used, as far as these are defined by the program, follow the principles laid down in the Concrete Society Publications *Standard Method of Detailing Reinforced Concrete*. Dimensions and bar descriptions are added to layouts and sections using the BASYS Programs previously described.

5.6 Design and Detailing of Building Services
The design of heating and ventilating systems involves the calculation of the loading from which package units can be chosen to provide the heating or cooling output required, and the sizing and balancing of ducting to ensure correct distribution of air or water flows.

82

No programs have yet been prepared for BASYS in this field, but work is in progress using the same hardware system—which may provide an important element for such a program. C. R. Dixon[5] is investigating the problems of pipework layout design with particular reference to testing for clashing in three-dimensional layouts. Although this work is intended primarily for chemical plant design, it is applicable to building services.

5.7 Other Systems

The BASYS System has been described in some detail in order to demonstrate the principles behind a computer draughting aid for designers. These same principles apply also to other systems which are being developed, although the mode of operation of these systems may differ from BASYS.

A very interesting example of such a system is the *Design Assistant* of Applicon, Inc. of Burlington, Massachusetts. It consists of a special desk into which is built a TEKTRONIX 611 Storage Tube, a keyboard, a data tablet and a PDP-11 computer. The PDP-11 is, of course, another Digital Equipment Corporation machine, one size larger than the PDP-8. The keyboard is similar to that of a teletype but without any output.

48
Design Assistant by Applicon Inc. The photograph shows the latest model which uses two storage tubes in the way described in the following texts.

The data tablet is a rectangular mesh of closely spaced fine wires covered with a plastic sheet. The tablet is the same size as the storage tube, and by pressing lightly on the plastic sheet with a special stylus, the position of the stylus can be registered on the storage tube screen as a moving spot in the same way as the movement of the joystick previously described. When, however, the operator exerts greater pressure, the main beam of the storage tube is activated and the movement of the stylus over the tablet is registered on the storage tube as a line.

Data is stored upon cassette tapes, two readers for which are built into the desk. The PDP-11 has 8K words (the PDP-11 uses 16 bit words). In addition, the system requires a small magnetic disc on which all the operating programs and data are held when working. The output can be to any available plotter, as it is claimed that software interfaces are available for all types. The working method with this system is similar to the BASYS System except that all new drawings are constructed on the storage tube instead of on a digitiser. Macros are stored on the disc by reading from a cassette tape, and are then scaled and orientated on the screen. The system is programmed so that the operator can input instructions to modify the data displayed on the screen by drawing simple symbols on the screen. The procedure in each case is to draw a diagonal line with the stylus across the item to be changed. A symbol such as a letter A, K or E is then drawn in the same way on any conveniently clear area of the screen, and the operation specified by the letter is performed on every item within the rectangle defined by the diagonal line. The operation may be, for example, to double the scale, rotate through ninety degrees or move to a different part of the screen.

Alternatively a menu can be displayed on the right-hand side of the screen and a selection made by pinpointing the required operation with the stylus. The menu takes the place of the symbols and provides a much larger range. In practice the two alternative methods are used together in much the same way as the menu and function buttons are used on the BASYS digitiser. The Applicon system costs about £35,000 ($85,000), the exact price being dependent upon the plotter and software provided.

Numerous systems are being developed both in Europe and America, and most involve a facility to display an image which has been stored on magnetic tape, and a means to modify the image and restore it. The TEKTRONIX Storage Tube display is, at present, the most popular means of doing this and some systems, like the one being developed at the Architectural Research Unit at the University of Edinburgh in Scotland, use two tubes. The ARV system uses a TEKTRONIX 4002A which consists of two storage tubes and a keyboard. The advantage of the twin-tube is that work can be carried out on one tube to modify parts of an overall image which is displayed on the other. In this way the operator can have a larger area of drawing displayed and extract a small part of it to the second tube, modify or detail the part, then return it to the original drawing to see how it fits. The system at present in use at Edinburgh uses a small computer (a Nova 800) which is linked to a large computer, a PDP-10, on a time-sharing system. The equipment is intended for research and is not considered to be an office operating system.

Several private practices in the United States and a local government office in England have developed systems using large computers to manipulate and plot a range of standard components. In general these offices have been concerned with designing standardized buildings using a limited range of pre-digitised components. The specialized systems they have developed on these large machines are of limited interest to the profession, but the pioneering work of these offices has been of great importance in the development of both the ideas and the hardware which are now being used in the developments described above.[11]

6 COMPUTERS IN DESIGN

6.1 Principles and Practice

This book has so far been largely concerned with aids to draughting and project organization, and the operating programs described have all been very small. The application of computers to aid design usually requires much larger programs, and with architectural design they can become very large indeed. Even with relatively small programs in this field, as the emphasis is usually towards logic and not arithmetic, the data handling problems can become formidable. This tends to make the processing of architectural programs rather expensive, so adding to the fundamental problem, namely that it is very difficult to assess the economic value to a practice of design programs.

The reason for this is best explained by comparison with applications in other fields. The structural engineers, for example, were one of the first to appreciate the capacities of the computer and for the last fifteen years or more have been using them to carry out calculations for their designs. Initially, the computer was used to replace the calculating machine and was valued largely for speed, economy and the reduction of the near menial labour required in such operations as inverting matrices. Later the capacity of the computer to perform calculations beyond the practical limits of human endeavour was appreciated, and some engineers have used this new power to build structures which previously could not safely be attempted.

Such programs operate usually to provide a solution to a problem which has one answer. Even if the cost of developing and running the program is quite high, its value can be compared to the cost of equivalent hand calculation or the building of an alternatively less advanced design.

When a computer aid is proposed to assist an architect, the object is somewhat different. Normally the intention is to provide him with an optimum solution to a part of his design problems which is amenable to a mathematical solution, or to provide him with the means of checking certain criteria which arise during the design which are otherwise cumbersome to handle unaided. Both these approaches can often be extended by allowing the computer to submit its own design solutions based on a limited number of criteria. These 'designs' can be seen either as providing a choice from which the architect can make his selection or as a preliminary investigation of the site's potential and a possible stimulus to the designer.

The first practical problem which arises when convincing an architect to use such a program is that it cannot be seen as replacing any specific part of the traditional design process which can be costed to check the economic value of its use. The only attempts so far made to provide figures for such an exercise have consisted of graphs which compare on one axis working days without a computer against, on the other axis, the number of working days one could afford for the same total expenditure when using a computer. Thus one can find, for example, that where it was expected that an assistant should spend forty working days on a design stage under normal conditions, if he should use a computer to aid him for a particular purpose, he should be able to work for twenty-three days without the costs of design rising. Inherent in such graphs is the not unreasonable assumption that the working time spent on a job is proportional to its size, as is the computer time required. What, however, is unreasonable is the assumption that the aid given to certain problems can be deducted from the overall time spent on the design.

Although computer programs can be produced which could be of great value to the architect, it is dangerous to consider them solely in terms of time savings. The architect designing a project does not leave it in the office when he goes home in the evening. Consciously or unconsciously, it is always with him and the passage of time is usually an important ingredient in shaping the qualities of his final design. Time spent at the drawing-board is no criterion in this respect, even if it is a recognized method of measuring output for the purpose of constructing time-tables. The purpose of the computer application is as an aid to improving the design or, as in engineering, to replacing menial routines or calculations. Such uses may save time, but it is doubtful whether this purpose could be justified as being of prime value to the architect.

The second problem which arises in the use of design programs is the limited extent to which architectural design is amenable to objective criteria. That is not to say that the objective criteria do not exist; in fact, they often appear to severely limit the architect's scope. However, when a computer is applied to the problem, the solutions possibly within the limits of these criteria alone are often so numerous that the cost of outputting them all could be prohibitive.

If an attempt is made to extend the program into the field of what could be called semi-objective criteria so as to reduce the numbers of solutions, the programming and running costs rise and the results become suspect. In the case, for example, of optimization, surprisingly simple problems by architects' standards can take a very long time to process and are totally uneconomic compared to normal methods—although the results may be very valuable. Too much importance, however, should not be placed upon these problems, for experience and new techniques of programming are already helping towards the solution of some of them and the next generation of computers, which will be with us before the end of this decade, should solve the running time problem.

Interactive graphics could be an important development in the architectural design field. The instrument for this work is normally the light pen described in 2.7. With such a system, the designer can interact with the program, applying alternatively his own criteria and those covered by the program. For some years teams have been working in many parts of the world developing techniques and programs for the light pen, but strikingly little design has ever been carried out using any of these systems. Again, cost is a major factor militating against its use.

The original systems all involved the operator working on line to the computer—which was quite impractical. More recent developments have resulted in the CRT being made self-sufficient as far as the preservation of the image is concerned, while the operation has become time sharing. The computer therefore is required only when a picture change or computation is carried out. Even on time sharing, however, the central computer time can be very expensive. The tube and light pen system is a major additional expense, and working close to a large cathode ray tube for any length of time is not to everyone's taste.

There are essentially two ways in which interactive graphics can be of value. First, the type of program which is capable of producing large numbers of objective solutions can, by interaction, be led to a single solution which satisfies the user. Second, optimization programs can be simplified and again given leads by the user who may, from experience, be able at least in part to predict a likely result. The danger here, of course, is that experience can be defined as that capacity which ensures that we repeat past mistakes consistently. It would in some respects be better to let the computer solve such problems unaided, although it is unwise to be pedantic on such a point as even the most abstract programs have built into them a great deal of human experience.

Most workers in the field of computer-aided architectural design would agree that the biggest obstruction to the wider use of such programs is the average architect's lack of access to a computer. It has been suggested that architects could be persuaded to hire computer time, attending a bureau to use the programs once these were available. This has always seemed unlikely to the author, who finds it difficult to visualize bureau visiting becoming a regular part of office routine unless the programs prove to be very powerful design tools indeed. This is unlikely to happen at an early stage, and so it is improbable that sufficient use could be made of such programs by practising architects for them to ever develop their full potential. The advent of the office operating system may be a significant factor in the development of computer-aided design, for it could provide means of access to a bureau machine through a terminal which is linked to the user's own equipment with which he is already familiar.

Many computer techniques could be applied to architectural design, but the work carried out so far has centred around three basic approaches, Optimization, Random Synthesis and Comparative Appraisal.

6.2 Planning by Optimization

Planning is the basic craft of architecture. The objective is always to arrange the items being planned in a way which best relates them to each other and to the conditions of the site. The related associations of each pair of items is normally predetermined, as are the conditions of the site; but, these factors alone may not result in a single plan, and other more subjective criteria are normally required to make a final choice.

This procedure is fundamental—from laying out furniture in a room to preparing a regional development plan for an entire nation. What we are concerned with in each case is a number of items of specifiable size, to be arranged in a given space and subject to certain controls. Some of the items may be further controlled in or near certain positions in the space, and some may need to be close to other items; that is to say, there is an association between such items and points of the site or between pairs of items.

With a simple problem like arranging furniture, the constraints are the dimensions of a room and possibly the need to have certain areas within it kept clear. The associations consist of such things as the need to have a reading-lamp near a certain chair, or a table adjacent to a couch or window. Once these constraints and associations have been listed, the room can be planned—although in practice it may prove necessary to relax some of the conditions in order to achieve an arrangement. To regularize this last move, it is possible to give each of the associations a rating dependent upon its importance. For instance, 10 if the two items should be adjacent to each other

Window
Armchair(1)
Armchair(2)
Reading lamp
Couch
Coffee Table
Piano

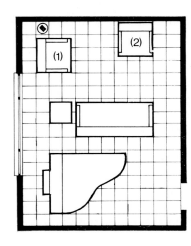

49
Simple room layout with possible chart of furniture associations

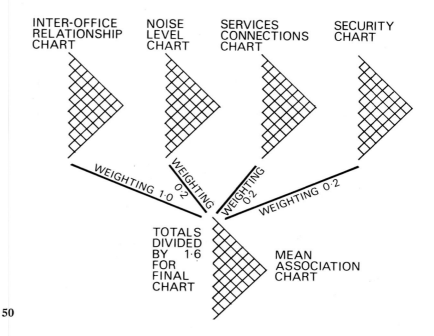

INTER-OFFICE RELATIONSHIP CHART

NOISE LEVEL CHART

SERVICES CONNECTIONS CHART

SECURITY CHART

WEIGHTING 1·0

WEIGHTING 0·2

WEIGHTING 0·2

WEIGHTING 0·2

TOTALS DIVIDED BY 1·6 FOR FINAL CHART

MEAN ASSOCIATION CHART

50

(i.e. chair and reading-lamp), and 7 if they need not be very close (i.e. chair and couch). These associations can be presented in chart form in which unrelated pairs of items (i.e. table and reading-lamp) have a zero rating. When in order to obtain a plan one or other of the associations must be waived, the one with the lowest rating is chosen.

Such a procedure is cumbersome for so small a planning problem, but when a building with many departments has to be planned it is much easier to separate the act of deciding how the departments are interrelated from that of actually preparing the layout. The giving of ratings to associations also turns a physical relationship into an arithmetical one, the significance of which should be obvious.

In such a system, the ratings 10 and 0 are absolute and indicate that the items concerned, whether they be departments or pieces of furniture, must in the first place be adjacent, and in the second place unrelated in any way. The allocation of values between these extremes is relative, so the significance lies not in whether the rating given to the association between A and B is 4 or 6, but whether relative to the ratings given to other associations, the assessment is appropriate.

If associations between items are for reasons which cannot in each case be conveniently compared, then several sets of intermediate associations can be developed and summed to give a total. The relative significance of each type of association, although difficult to relate to individual cases, can often be assessed as an overall principle and allowed for by deciding a weighting. The weighting from 0·1 to 1·0 in ten equal steps is multiplied by each association before they are summed. The departments in an office building, for example, might be associated primarily by the inter-office relationships—director to manager, secretary to typist, manager to drawing office, etc. They can also be related by noise levels, connections with services and security. After deciding the associations between each pair of departments for each of the four types of association, it may be decided that, for example, the inter-office relationship is of much greater significance than any of the others. So a weighting of 1·0 is given to it, and perhaps 0·2 to the other three. The maximum rating for the final association is thus 16 (i.e. $10 \times 1·0 + 10 \times 0·2 + 10 \times 0·2 + 10 \times 0·2 = 16$. All the values obtained therefore can be normalized, i.e. brought back to a fraction of 10 by dividing them all by 1·6. The final value obtained is called the 'mean' association.

The primary stages of planning are now in a suitable form for computer handling. To proceed further, it is necessary to determine the constraints defining the area upon which the planning is to take place. These constraints can be the walls of a room or the boundaries and existing features of a site. In

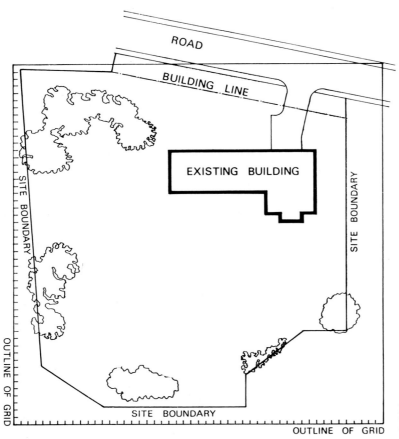

51
Plan of site with outline of grid superimposed

92

52
Site plan transferred to grid showing locations occupied by existing building, trees and site limits

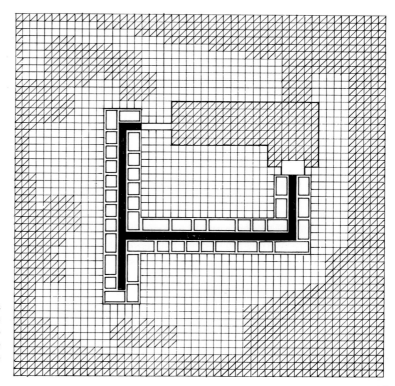

53
Proposed disposition of rooms in new building. Circulation axis is predetermined and rooms positioned in order, starting with those having the maximum association to the existing building

either case, the simplest way to handle the definition of such a space is by a grid.

A grid in a program can be dimensionless and the size chosen to suit any particular problem. The site can be defined by the grid simply by storing in the computer details of each grid location. Such details will indicate in the simplest manner whether or not the location is within the site and whether or not there is a tree or existing building already upon it.

Consider a grid upon which has been positioned three items, 1, 2 and 3. Assume that each item will fit on a single grid and the locations chosen have already been selected as suitable. If a fourth item is now positioned on the grid, and two alternative positions considered, the relative suitability of each may be assessed by comparing the values for the mean associations of the new item with each of the existing items.

The larger the mean association, the smaller the distance between the associated items should be; that is to say, the summation of each mean association multiplied by its relevant distance should be minimized. The best position would thus have the lowest value of Q where—

$$Q = A_{14}d_{14} + A_{24}d_{24} + A_{34}d_{34}$$

and A_{14} is the mean association of, and d_{14} is the distance between item 1 and item 4. This value Q can be calculated for numerous positions of item 4, and the item's best position determined as that for which Q is minimum.

The above procedure can be set up as a computer program in which the values for each of the intermediate associations is stored as a matrix of numbers, and the site grid as a similar matrix which specifies the shape of the site and the positions of any fixed objects. The weightings of each intermediate matrix can be specified, and the mean associations automatically computed. The program can then search the intermediate association matrix for items with absolute associations to fixed points of the site which the designer should clearly position first, and then list all the remaining items in a declining order of association from these first selected items.

This list prepared by summing the intermediate associations will provide a guide to the order in which the positioning of the items can best be attempted. The designer should now try to position the items on the site in the given order. Each time a position is proposed for a given item, the value of Q is calculated automatically and compared with previously tried positions. The minimum value of Q obtained indicates the best position. In practice items need not all be of single grid size but can cover a block of grids. In such cases the program will take the distance between the centres of the blocks.

Such a program can be extended in a number of different ways. A series of site grid matrices can be prepared, each of which specifies the quality of the site at each location regarding a particular characteristic. For example, with a typical building site, a matrix could be prepared to show relative foundation costs—or another to show the variation of noise level from adjacent roads. A mean grid value N can be automatically prepared, using a series of weightings to account for the varying importance of the different factors. The value for Q can then be modified by the value obtained for the average mean grid value N for the grid locations upon which the item being checked is located. Having decided the various associations and site grids and obtained from the program a list of items in planning order, it should be possible in theory to start placing items on the site while checking all possible alternative positions to obtain the lowest value of QN.

In the case of a very simple problem involving not more than about a dozen items, this method is likely to provide an answer; but for a much larger and complex problem, it is almost certain to result in a design which is later re-shaped around more coherent circulation axes.

A further extension to the program therefore is to determine before starting the major circulation routes around which planning should take place. Once this is done, a further site grid can be constructed to specify the routes, and a value for each grid location which indicates how near it is to a route established. A further association is then decided for each item, indicating whether or not it needs to be near a route. The circulation site grid and the circulation association matrix are used to obtain the circulation rating for any proposed location.

From this point, it is a comparatively simple step to make the whole process automatic. Thus the program selects each item in the order specified by the intermediate matrices, sums the mean association for each in turn and uses it to calculate the QN value for every possible grid or group of grids on to which the item could fit. The values thus obtained are used with the circulation rating of each location to choose an optimum position. This procedure is repeated for each item in turn, until either the last is located or else a point is reached at which an item cannot be positioned.

When this happens, it is normally due to the fact that the item in question has an association which requires it to be adjacent to another item which has already been positioned in the development in such a way that there is no suitable location for the original item. In this event, the item in question is moved automatically to an earlier position in the listing initially prepared from the intermediate matrices, and the planning is started afresh.

When a first result is obtained, the designer can assess it and by modifying either the association values, weightings or circulation pattern, cause a re-run to produce a different layout. The program can be developed further to allow for multi-storey buildings and for the open spaces required in front of the windows. This brief description outlines the method of working for such a program. More detailed descriptions have been published elsewhere.[12]

6.3 BAID-1 and Random Synthesis

The Basic Architectural Investigation and Design Program One is an aid to the design of medium- and high-density housing layouts. It was conceived by the author and developed with the assistance of the staff of the Computer-Aided Design Workshop in the Department of Engineering at the University of Leicester, England. It is planned to be the first of a series of architectural design aids which it is hoped will be developed at the workshop.

This program resulted from a search carried out in the mid-sixties for a viable alternative to high-rise building for high-density housing. It was concluded that an economic alternative did exist in the form of medium-rise three to five storey developments, but that the planning controls necessary for such designs were difficult and time-consuming to apply. It was also found that much building in this field was often repetitive and uninteresting largely because of the apparently limited possibilities. The planning controls referred to, as applied in Britain, set minimum values for the amount of daylight and sunlight which could fall upon the windows of a dwelling, and upon the spacing of dwellings to obtain privacy between opposing windows.

Such limitations appear both logical and reasonable, and when used on small developments allow ample scope for variations. On large developments, however, the controls seem to apply a significant brake upon efforts to introduce variation between groupings. To aid this situation, it was decided to develop a computer program to apply the planning constraints referred to, so that the designer could plan the site and be informed automatically if the introduction of a dwelling or a block of dwellings resulted in a contravention of the regulations.

For this purpose, the constraints adopted were those normally applied by Local Planning Authorities in Britain with the support of the Ministry of Housing. The criteria and regulations are as follows:

1 The amount of daylight falling on each façade in the manner determined by the Ministry of Housing indicators.

2 The minimum hours of sunlight falling on the living-room façade during ten months of the year.

3 The distance between windows of different dwellings, to assess the compliance within the minimum figure required for privacy. By setting specified values in the data relating to 1 for percentage of sky visible, and 2 for hours of sunlight, the designs produced could satisfy the requirements for British Standards Code of Practice No. 3, Chapter 1, Part 1A Daylighting and

Chapter 1B Sunlighting. By setting limits for 3 to comply with Table 15 of the Scottish Building Regulations, the designs produced could satisfy these regulations regarding window privacy. The Scottish Building Regulations provide a refined method of assessing this factor, and should satisfy all local authorities in Britain.

In Britain the planning controls are quite clearly defined, and it is standard practice for local authorities to require that any high-density development should be shown to comply with the above rules. The validity of these three rules is, of course, open to question. They are used in this program for two reasons.

First, when applied to established developments they are often viable, and where not so it usually appears that it is the excessively high standard they set rather than the principles on which they are based that is at fault. The neighbourly relationships which exist in a democratic society normally dictate that no one should build so as to seriously obstruct the light of his neighbour, block out the sun completely, or place a wall so close to his windows as to deprive him of the view. Mutually agreed principles have therefore developed into regulations even if the standards are now somewhat higher.

Second, the application of these rules in the program is only as a means of control. No one rule is indispensable to it, and the influence of each can be varied by modifying the controlling values. Thus whether or not the actual values required to satisfy the Planning Controls are used, the criteria are a measure of at least some of the qualities which are relevant to the assessment of any housing layout.

At about the time this program was first conceived, the author was asked to investigate the possibility of developing a small island off the coast of Calabria, Italy. The development was a holiday town of about 1,500 dwellings with an hotel, marina, etc. The ground was to remain in the ownership of the holding company and the dwellings sited freely on the landscaped rocky sides of the island. A prefabricated unit was designed which was supported by a space frame structure which rested at only a limited number of points, and a range of different dwellings devised from combinations of these units.

The siting of the dwellings then became the central problem. The subjects of daylight and sunlight were unimportant in Calabria—the relevant qualities required in this situation being privacy and a clear view of the sea. The program described in flowchart form in 3.5 is a simplified version of what was required. The intention initially was to choose a series of sites for 50×50 squares of a 2 m grid on an aerial survey of the island, using stereoscopic prints to level each grid location. It was then proposed that these squares should be developed in turn with a predefined number of dwellings, and the landscaping designed to suit the resulting scheme.

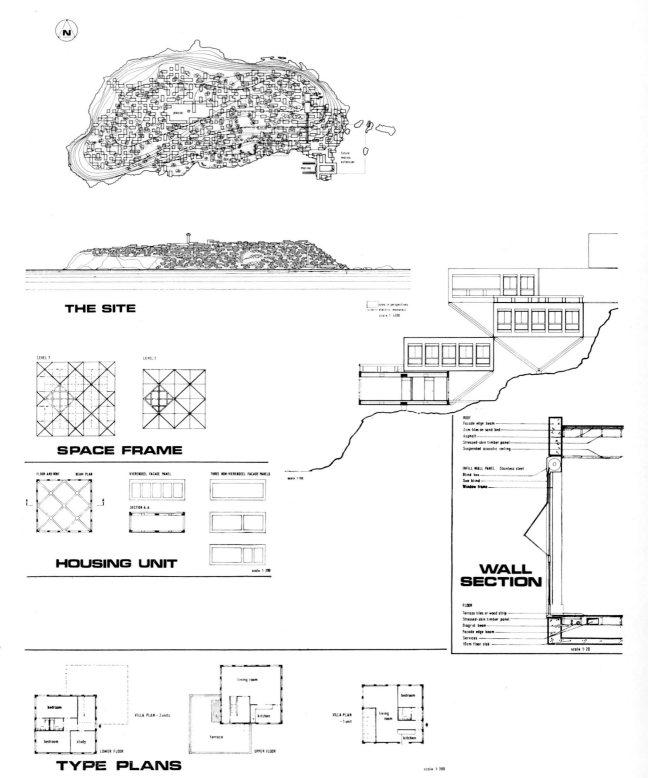

THE SITE

area in perspectives
electric monorail
scale 1: 4000

SPACE FRAME

LEVEL 1   LEVEL 2

HOUSING UNIT

FLOOR AND ROOF   BEAM PLAN   VIERENDEEL FACADE PANEL   THREE NON-VIERENDEEL FACADE PANELS

SECTION A-A

scale 1:200

scale 1:100

WALL
SECTION

ROOF
Facade edge beam
2cm tiles on sand bed
Asphalt
Stressed-skin timber panel
Suspended acoustic ceiling

INFILL WALL PANEL Stainless steel
Blind box
Sun blind
Window frame

FLOOR
Terrazo tiles or wood strip
Stressed-skin timber panel
Diagrid beam
Facade edge beam
Services
10cm floor slab

scale 1:20

TYPE PLANS

bedroom
bedroom   study
LOWER FLOOR

VILLA PLAN - 2 units

living room
kitchen
terrace
UPPER FLOOR

VILLA PLAN - 1 unit

bedroom
living room
kitchen

scale 1:200

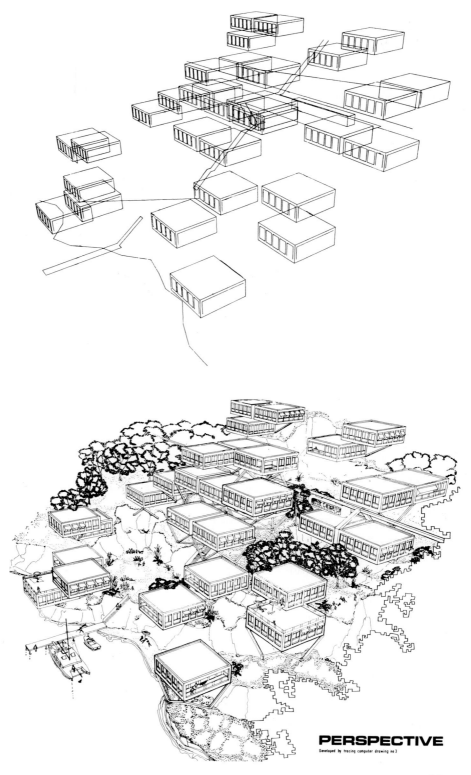

54
Isola Dino Project.
Proposed holiday
development of an
island off the coast of
Calabria. The housing
units were to be
precast in concrete and
suspended in a space
frame over the rocky
sloping surface of the
island. The multi-layer
space frame, also in
precast concrete, has
diagonals in alternate
bays, thus permitting
a cuboid to be placed
diagonally between the
frame members, the
cuboid in this case
being the housing unit.
Each dwelling is made
up of a combination of
units, one, two or
three, either side by
side or inter-related
upon different levels.
The space frame
geometry dictates the
relationship which can
be seen clearly on the
two unit dwelling in
the foreground of the
perspective. Plans of
the one unit and two
unit dwellings are
included. A proposed
layout for a part of the
site drawn by the
plotter is shown on
the right and below
it a developed
perspective prepared
by tracing over the
plotter output

PERSPECTIVE

Developed by tracing computer drawing no 3

It was found in practice, however, that working on the bare rocky surface resulted in a freedom of action so wide that a near random distribution of dwellings was possible. From this arose the concept of the automatic generation of random layouts. The random number table is a mathematical device used in statistical calculations. It consists of lists of groups of digits which are chosen at random by methods which resemble a roulette table in their action. Many computer programs have been devised to generate random numbers, and the problem of obtaining large quantities of numbers in which no relationship can be traced is one of quite surprising complexity. In this case, however, only a very short list of numbers was required and a simple generator was able to serve the purpose.

What was finally proposed for the Isola Dino Project was that a program should be prepared which would generate six-digit random numbers, and then site a dwelling using the first two to determine the grid position x coordinate, the second two to determine the grid position y coordinate, the fifth digit the height above ground level, and the sixth to determine the dwelling type to be used. Once two dwellings had been sited in this way, the positions chosen could be checked to ensure that neither obstructed the view of the other. If there was an obstruction, the second position was to be rejected and a new random number generated to determine a new position and the checks repeated.

Once a satisfactory position was found, a third dwelling could be introduced and checked relative to the first two. This process was continued until the required number of dwellings was sited on the grid. The whole process of choosing and checking was to be carried out by the computer which would thus be preparing 'designs'. If the result was not to the liking of the designer, he simply repeated the program to obtain a further 'design'.

The Isola Dino Project was shelved for financial reasons, but the idea of using random numbers to produce 'designs' was included in the BAID-1 Program.[13] In its latest form the BAID-1 Program requires a designer to layout his site on a grid, choosing the grid size to suit the size of the site. The exact size of the grid is also related to a pad size. The pad is a square of grids normally between three grids and five grids square, into which each dwelling type to be used must fit in plan. Pads can be of one or two storeys each, and can be assembled in towers to any height, the limit being specified in the data. If, having chosen a pad size, the grid will not cover the site, then the site should be developed in two parts or more. The procedure to be followed when using the program is shown in the flowchart in Figure 55, the stages of which are as follows:

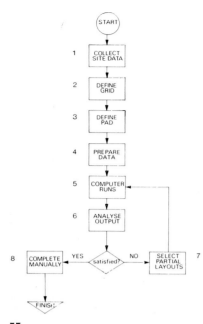

55
BAID Flowchart

1 Site Data Collection
The first task of the designer is to collect data defining the boundaries and contours of his site, and to list all the constraints which restrict buildings on it, e.g. existing houses, trees, roads, etc.

2 Grid Definition
Positions on the site are located by means of a 99×99 square grid. The designer must select the most suitable orientation for this grid and ensure that its size is larger than the site or part of the site which it is proposed to plan.

3 Pad Definition
Information describing the various types of dwellings to be built, such as their dimensions, position of their windows, etc., is used by the designer to define 'the pads'. The pad has two opposite sides which are assumed glazed, and the direction perpendicular to this glazing is called the pad's orientation.

4 Data Preparation
At this stage the data are prepared in a form acceptable to a computer using standard data sheets. Data input to the computer defines the portions of the site on which building is permitted and describes the various types of dwellings. It also specifies a number of parameters such as the elevation of the sun for the latitude of the site, or the percentage of sky, hours of sunlight and privacy distances required.

5 Computer Runs
The data and the program are fed to the computer which produces a number of original layouts for the site. At this stage the time-consuming work has been performed by the machine and the designer can assess the results.

6 Output Analysis
The designer uses his own judgement and his sense of order and aesthetics to analyse the computer-produced layouts. If he is sufficiently satisfied with these results, he can complete his work unaided.

7 Manual Completion
When the layout of the pads is finalized, the design must be completed by choosing the position and type of dwelling to be used on each pad, and all necessary access (stairs, lifts) must be sited within the outline of each block of pads.

8 Freezing Capability
If the designer is not satisfied with the computer output, he selects some portions of the site which are of interest, modifies them manually as he sees fit and freezes them. He can now use the computer to re-plan the remaining areas of the site.

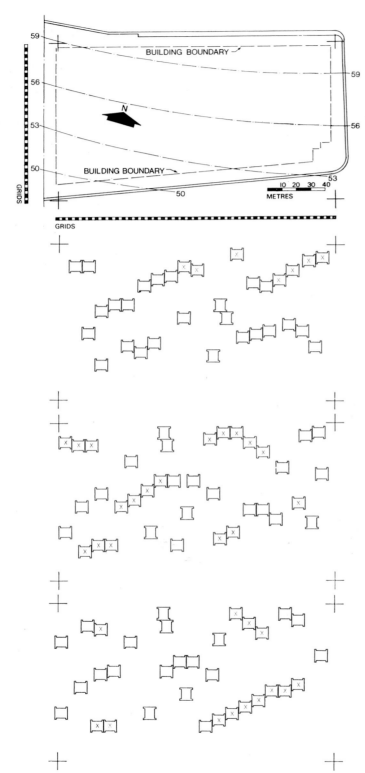

The diagrams on the left are the BAID Program for the site shown at the top of the page. The four crosses are for location purposes, the one bottom left being at grid reference $x=1$, $y=1$. Each rectangle is a pad the window faces of which are shown as an inset panel on the face. The grid size is 2·3 m and each pad is four grids or 9·2 m square. Each block of pads is either three or four storeys high and each layout, produced of course as a random distribution, complies with the British planning law regarding daylight, sunlight, and privacy. Each pad in fact has a minimum of 1 per cent of the sky visible at every point on each window face, this percentage being viewed through a standard aperture which ensures adequate light at the back of each room. It also has a minimum of two hours of sunlight for ten months of the year falling on the full width of one window face and no window face is closer than 18·3 m (70 ft) to any directly opposing window face. Because the site slopes quite steeply from north to south a strong bias (possibly too strong) was given to the selection of y–y orientations. This ensured that most chains formed along the contours and not across them which would be more difficult and expensive to build.

The author, after a few minutes' study of the three layouts, produced the sketch design shown top right. The object of producing the random generated layouts is to stimulate the designer's imagination, give him a sense of scale for the site and provide him with possible ideas for groupings etc. It is not intended that he should necessarily use the exact locations on any of the random layouts on his final scheme. In this case, however, to help show the influence of the random generated layouts many locations have been transfered and those used have been marked with an X on each of the original runs. The design sketch is intended to show how the author visualized a scheme using some of the locations from each random generated run plus a few extra of his own choosing to provide a layout in which the dwellings have:

a. Outlooks of varying distance from most windows.

b. Adequate open space and pedestrian links throughout the site.

c. Vehicular access to points on the site which comply with local authority requirements for delivery services and refuse collection.

The sketch design was fed back to the computer to produce the final layout shown centre right and the data print-out below right. The data is in tabular form as follows, reading from left to right. First is the pad number followed by the x and y coordinate (in grids) values and under z the ordinance datum level (in metres) of the ground floor slab. Under the heading ORIENTATION is given the direction in which the window faces are orientated and the word 'small' or 'large' indicating the height of the block, in this case either three or four storeys. The PERCENTAGE SKY VISIBLE is given at each edge and at the centre of each window face and the SUN TIME IN MINUTES for the same positions but only for the face nearest to south.

The print-out also includes a list (not reproduced) of pads which do not satisfy the checks fully. With the random generated runs such locations would be rejected automatically, but for a set of locations submitted by a designer the program accepts all, states which ones do not comply, and leaves the designer to check the acceptability of his particular dwelling designs in each location himself.

The computer drawings are reproduced directly from the drum plotter output and the data from the line printer copy.

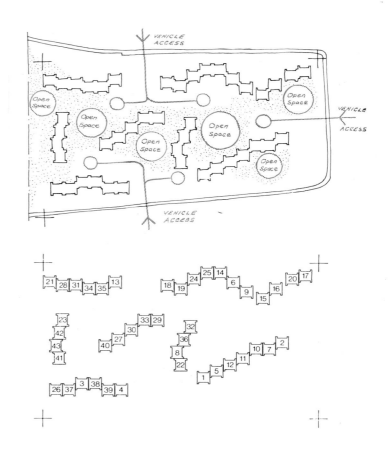

PAD	X	Y	Z	ORIENT	SIZE	PERCENTAGE SKY VISIBLE						SUN TIMES IN MINUTES					
43	3	22	53.90	XX	SMALL	2.443	5.165	2.411	5.659	5.659	5.659	0	0	0	437	437	437
42	4	26	55.30	XX	SMALL	2.547	5.205	5.237	2.857	5.659	5.659	0	0	0	402	437	
41	4	16	52.60	XX	SMALL	4.809	4.839	4.646	5.659	5.659	2.857	0	0	0	437	437	437
40	14	22	54.80	YY	SMALL	5.659	5.659	5.659	4.425	4.490	2.075	762	783	783	0	0	0
39	19	8	50.40	YY	SMALL	5.659	5.659	5.659	1.312	3.315	3.281	783	783	783	0	0	0
38	15	10	50.30	YY	SMALL	2.857	5.659	5.659	2.994	2.861	2.634	423	783	743	0	0	0
37	7	8	50.20	YY	SMALL	5.659	5.659	3.157	2.929	0.905		743	783	743	0	0	0
36	42	24	55.30	XX	SMALL	2.597	5.019	4.824	2.056	4.043	3.313	0	0	0	254	374	
35	17	46	58.40	YY	SMALL	5.530	5.606	5.651	5.659	5.659	2.857	614	642	649	0	0	0
34	13	40	58.30	YY	SMALL	5.648	5.612	5.465	2.857	5.659	5.659	635	635	565	0	0	0
33	30	30	56.70	YY	SMALL	5.637	4.959	2.857	4.177	3.990	3.626	712	592	345	0	0	0
32	44	20	56.70	XX	SMALL	5.028	5.155	5.195	1.324	3.709	3.481	0	0	0	216	352	
31	9	41	59.20	YY	SMALL	2.834	5.577	5.494	5.659	5.659	5.659	367	783	783	0	0	0
30	26	34	56.70	YY	SMALL	5.659	4.959	2.857	4.378	4.122	2.305	564	656	712	0	0	0
29	34	30	56.70	YY	SMALL	4.996	5.529	5.637	3.626	3.216	2.358	783	635	360	0	0	0
28	5	41	59.00	YY	SMALL	5.449	5.407	5.449	2.857	5.659	5.659	783	783	769	0	0	0
27	22	24	55.10	YY	SMALL	5.659	5.659	5.659	4.231	3.825	1.946	743	783	360	0	0	0
26	3	0	50.10	YY	SMALL	5.659	5.659	5.659	3.207	3.251	3.151	743	783	783	0	0	0
25	49	45	59.50	YY	LARGE	5.659	5.652	2.857	5.659	5.659	5.659	776	727	360	0	0	0
24	45	43	59.50	YY	LARGE	5.644	4.930	2.835	5.659	5.659	2.857	741	635	360	0	0	0
23	5	30	55.30	XX	LARGE	4.671	4.988	5.070	2.857	5.659	5.659	0	0	0	402	437	
22	41	16	53.40	XX	SMALL	3.333	2.348	1.636	5.474	5.326	2.857	0	0	0	385	437	437
21	1	42	59.00	YY	SMALL	2.852	5.618	5.651	5.659	5.659	5.659	423	769	712	0	0	0
20	75	43	59.50	YY	SMALL	5.659	5.659	2.857	5.659	5.659	2.857	743	727	508	0	0	0
19	41	40	59.00	YY	LARGE	5.257	5.156	4.962	2.857	4.959	2.857	649	494	360	0	0	0
18	37	41	59.50	YY	LARGE	2.622	5.213	4.997	5.659	5.659	5.659	204	480	522	0	0	0
17	79	46	59.50	YY	SMALL	5.659	5.659	2.857	5.659	5.659	5.659	743	783	360	0	0	0
16	70	46	59.30	YY	SMALL	5.647	4.936	2.846	5.659	5.659	3.989	783	635	360	0	0	0
15	66	37	59.00	YY	SMALL	5.428	5.412	5.428	4.474	4.959	2.857	783	783	755	0	0	0
14	53	45	59.50	YY	LARGE	2.857	4.959	5.659	5.659	5.659	5.659	423	691	776	0	0	0
13	21	42	59.50	YY	LARGE	5.586	5.647	2.857	5.659	5.659	5.659	670	656	317	0	0	0
12	56	16	53.70	YY	LARGE	5.659	5.659	2.857	4.489	4.610	2.544	743	727	360	0	0	0
11	60	16	53.70	YY	LARGE	5.659	5.659	2.857	4.236	3.614	2.280	783	727	360	0	0	0
10	64	21	55.40	YY	LARGE	5.659	4.959	2.857	3.806	3.761	3.700	783	635	360	0	0	0
9	61	34	59.00	YY	SMALL	4.404	5.613	5.635	2.857	5.659	5.659	635	783	748	0	0	0
8	40	20	53.50	XX	SMALL	1.968	4.201	2.622	5.029	4.684	4.092	0	0	0	437	437	437
7	68	21	55.40	YY	LARGE	5.659	5.659	5.659	3.700	3.743	1.549	743	783	783	0	0	0
6	57	42	59.50	YY	LARGE	2.857	4.959	5.659	2.857	4.959	5.659	402	656	734	0	0	0
5	52	14	52.50	YY	LARGE	5.659	5.659	2.857	3.787	4.219	2.228	783	727	360	0	0	0
4	23	8	50.50	YY	SMALL	5.659	5.659	5.659	3.315	3.338	3.413	783	743	783	0	0	0
3	11	10	50.50	YY	SMALL	5.659	5.659	2.857	2.803	2.953	2.994	743	727	360	0	0	0
2	72	25	55.40	YY	LARGE	5.659	5.659	2.857	3.074	3.423	3.767	783	727	360	0	0	0
1	48	12	52.40	YY	LARGE	5.659	5.659	5.659	2.993	3.746	1.775	783	783	783	0	0	0

The print-out from the program is on a drum plotter and provides plans and sections and/or an axonometric of each layout prepared. A fully interactive version of this program has also been prepared in which the operator obtains an outline of the site and grid upon a CRT and can site pads with a light pen. He can also allow a random number generator to position pads and he can eliminate, before it is checked, any pad of which he does not approve the position. The random positioning can be limited to within specified areas, and at any point in the proceedings the operator can add or subtract pads from the screen.

The operation of this version, including orders to print-out in various forms, is carried out entirely by the use of the light pen and the function key buttons on the CRT. When the layouts are prepared entirely by random number generation, it is assumed that the user will prepare several 'designs' and use these as a preliminary investigation of the site, and as a stimulus to his own ideas.

The use of a random number generator to simulate a designer may at first sight appear a rather crude device. It became apparent, however, when attempting to plan on the bare rocky slopes of Isola Dino, that with a simple predefined objective and practically no obstructions the first 'act of choice' when attempting to find a suitable location was indeed a very random one. The eye travelled rapidly over the paper selecting possible locations at random, after which an approximate check by eye led one to either consider the location further or move on.

When a more complex site is being planned, this random search is only a small part of the procedure and tends to be overlooked; but it does exist, and without it the process of designing would probably be impossible. When a complex site is being planned with the full BAID-1 Program using the random number generator, the time taken to select a number is very small and, in proportion to the remainder of the process, must be roughly in scale to the random eye movement period in the normal design process.

After selecting a position using a random number, the program does a high-speed check to decide if the location proposed seems practical. This check may result in the pad being rotated or moved according to a simple set of rules which orientate the new pad to others in its immediate vicinity which have previously been accepted. Each accepted pad has a 'zone' over which it exerts control to ensure that lengthy checks are not carried out on irrationally placed pads. The degree to which such controls are applied is preset by the user who can vary the zone size to give the degree of control he requires.

Another aspect of the use of random numbers in this context which is of interest is their potential for simulating natural growth. Much of the dissatisfaction expressed by the inhabitants of new towns and other large housing developments concerns the visual quality of their environment, which is compared unfavourably to that of adjacent older towns. The individuality of these older areas is their principal virtue, and this stems largely from a continual development over hundreds of years, in which each dwelling has evolved to suit the needs of its owners and the constraints of its neighbours. By comparison, the modern development is usually planned in a short period as an entity to which little can be added. It seems possible that with the computer's capacity to compress into a few minutes many lifetimes of analysis, something of the character and variation which long-established developments possess might be simulated to assist in new designs. Random Synthesis appears reasonable in this case, as the growth or rebuilding of each dwelling in a long-established group has normally taken place at intervals over generations, at times dictated by birth, death, fire and financial success, all somewhat random occurrences.

6.4 Comparative Appraisal

This is a follow-up technique to the two described in 6.2 and 6.3, in that whereas previously we were concerned with producing designs, Comparative Appraisal, as its name suggests, is concerned with appraising a design by comparison with a previously assessed corpus of similar projects. The design involved need not have been otherwise aided by a computer, although if it had been the output data of the previous program would be directly applicable as appraisal program input.

Such a program could be used to appraise the relative merits of designs produced using BAID-1 for example, by comparing similar schemes for a given site to determine which had the lowest percentage of dwellings to come within, say, ten per cent of all the minimum values specified for the three criteria. It could also assess other factors not considered in the original program. For example, it could sum the total external wall space of the blocks on each scheme as an assessment of the likely comparative heating costs.

When buildings not designed with a program such as BAID-1 are to be appraised, each design must first be specified —usually on a grid so as to make possible the coding of all the parts of it which are relevant to the criteria being assessed. As long as the designs being appraised are comparable, that is to say designed to the same or very similar conditions and specification, the appraisal should be simply direct comparisons such as floor space per bed for hospital wards or average front door to car space distance in housing. Such appraisal programs can compare any number of criteria, and can be planned in an extendable form, so that an additional criterion can be added when its importance is appreciated or a means of programming discovered.

Such programs could be used to aid jurors assess a competition by providing accurate comparative data on the entries, or they could be used by medical and educational boards to assess the material advantages involved in a new design of a hospital or school. To do this it would, of course, be necessary to build up a data bank of existing buildings against which comparisons could be made.

Comparative Appraisal is not such an obviously original technique as either of the previous two described, but it could prove ultimately to be of much greater significance. Man's search for theoretical explanations is, at least where technology is concerned, an attempt on the part of the individual to by-pass experience. The designer who does not have a satisfactory theory must either have experience of very similar work, or be advised by one who has—otherwise the risk of failure is very great. In very few fields can personal experience be entirely dispensed with, but in those where the work of others is well documented, the individual has much greater freedom. The computer techniques of comparative appraisal, although still at a very early stage, appear to represent a higher order of documentation than previously available and may revolutionize our concepts of human learning.[14]

6.5 Experiment in Architecture

A client commissioning an architect expects him to be conversant with recent advances in architectural theory and building technology, and to make full use of this knowledge, but he does not usually expect him to risk untried methods. He may, however, be prepared to accept and in some cases actually request that the architect should experiment with the design and consider original methods of building, and he may even choose his architect because of his reputation for successful experimentation.

When he does this, it is usually with the objective of either reducing costs or building time, overcoming or exploiting the characteristic of the site, using materials which he wishes to see exploited, not using others in short supply, gaining prestige for himself and/or the building, or a combination of several of these objectives.

The last of these, prestige, is probably the most common reason that experiment is actually sought by the client, while the first, cost reduction, is the most frequent cause of his having it thrust upon him.

For many architects the opportunity to experiment is highly prized, and for some it is the prime objective—yet experiment in architecture can be a dangerous business. Experimental designs are obviously more liable to failure, both as designs and as buildings. Costly litigation and high indemnity insurance are the principal risks and an unbuilt project the most common outcome. This is due, in part, to the fact that as an experimenter today's architect is in a very weak position. The architect's method of designing is one of intuitive investigation in a field which has the minimum of objective criteria. He is not trained in the scientific method, and if he were, it would be of little value to him as a designer because there is rarely time for research. Research is a particular form of experiment in which intuition and creative skill is used to construct an hypothesis which is then investigated scientifically with the object of proving or disproving it. In architecture, what might be called the artistic method is used. This consists of studying the existing facts and deducing from them a supposedly self-evident hypothesis which is then demonstrated as a work of art.

To guarantee success with this method, both the facts and deductions must be true, while it is the very nature of experiment that they must be open to question. The deductions required are made during the design process, and at this stage the architect should have self-confidence before experimenting. If he is heavily dependent upon sub-consultants, his biggest problem will be knowing when his own knowledge is deficient, and even with specialists' advice there is always the risk of an unforeseen secondary effect. For the facts, he is dependent upon others and here the information can be inaccurate or he may wrongly interpret facts which have been originally obtained for other purposes.

Because he is not trained in the scientific method, the architect is not equipped to carry out technical research and much of the money now being used by schools to introduce post-graduate research will be wasted if this fact is not better appreciated. The architect's office is also totally unsuited for re-search development into materials and production methods for which he must be dependent upon research stations and indus-tries. The architect's field for research is in initiating hypotheses and devising applications. Thus the architect should use his own experimental methods to conceive better solutions to his architectural problems. He should then pass on to industry the technical problems so produced, and apply himself to the task of exploiting the results. It is rarely possible within a single building project, however, for the architect to carry out both aspects of this participation, as there is no time between them for the industrial research and development to be performed. Thus the experimental designs which are never intended to be built but which investigate hypotheses and propose solutions are a very important aspect of architecture and probably the best field for post-graduate studies.

If there is close cooperation between an architect and a large industrial concern with advanced research facilities, it is sometimes possible to develop a building technique within a single project. An example of this type of experiment was the author's Gyrotron Structures at Expo '67, Montreal, Canada. This was not a National Pavilion but a centrepiece for the light entertainment area of the exhibition.[15] The structures contained two enclosed spaces through which passed a fairground ride.

The larger structure was required to contain an enclosed space of a million cubic feet and was the highest building in the entire exhibition. As the budget for this structure was approximately $650,000, that is to say 65 cents per cubic foot, it had to be built using the minimum of materials. At the rates then current in Canada for fabricated and assembled materials in high buildings, this represented only about half a pound of aluminium or a pound and a quarter of steel for each cubic foot of contained space for both structure and cladding. At the same time, the size and location required that the structure should be of interest and an attraction to the public using the area.

A space frame structure was designed and tenders called for both in steel and aluminium. Full details were provided for the member sizes, and several alternative jointing systems proposed from which the contractor could choose. A tender using aluminium was the lowest and this was accepted.

A full analysis of the aluminium structure was then carried out using the computer program STAR. Simultaneously the principal contractor undertook a detailed study of the structural characteristics of the members, joints and cladding. The results were closely studied by the authorities concerned, and it was agreed that the detailed computer analysis and structural investigation provided sufficient evidence of the safety of the proposal to permit such a lightweight structure to be built. The final weight of the large building was just over seven ounces per cubic foot of enclosed space, probably the lightest rigid structure of its size ever constructed.

The risk of unforeseen secondary effects in such experiments is always present. The possibility of wind-excited oscillation of the tubular members of the space frame was foreseen, and a size chosen to prevent the known forms of resonance occurring. A completely new mode of oscillation was discovered, however, which had never before been seen on a structure. The principal contractor's research company investigated this problem on the smaller structure which had been built first out of prudence and were able to propose a cure before the main structure was erected. The installation of several hundred stockbridge dampers solved the problem at a very reasonable cost, and no further vibration was experienced.[16] Although designed for the exhibition, the Gyrotron Structures, like many other buildings on the site, are still standing.

A number of writers have attempted to link modern architecture more closely to modern scientific thought by proposing an association between architectural theory and Einstein's

63
Plan and Elevation of Gyrotron Structures

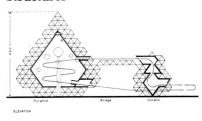

64
**The Gyroton Structures floodlit
at night. Only a night shot can
reproduce in a black and white
photograph the contrast obtained
in daylight between the aluminium tubes of the structure and
the deep blue summer sky of
Montreal**

Theory of Relativity, by reference to space-time and the fourth
dimension. No association has ever been shown and nothing has
actually come of these ideas except a revised interest in one of
the earliest architectural visual techniques, namely parallax.[17]
The exposed space frame of the Gyrotron was, as a further
experiment, shaped to emphasize the parallax effects which
can be obtained with such multi-membered structures. As it
was possible to walk under the overhanging sides of the
structures, parallax was visible in all dimensions. Listening to
the comments of the passing crowds, it was evident that many
visitors were made conscious of this ancient visual experience
for possibly the first time in their lives.

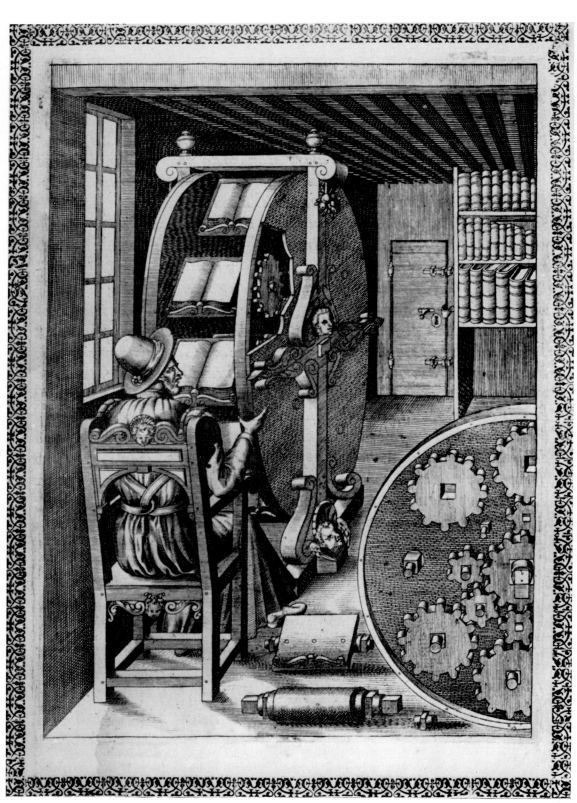

7 PROSPECTS AND CONCLUSIONS

7.1 Hardware Developments

It is hoped that the reader will feel that this book has justified the assertions made in the first chapter regarding the future importance to the profession of the computer. This is a rapidly developing field, in which costs are falling steadily and expertise is rising. More sophisticated techniques of data handling are likely to appear in the next few years which should go a long way towards solving the present problems of hardware operation and design program development.

The changing shape of the computer industry would appear to favour the smaller users like the professions. The building industry has been a disappointment to the big computer companies who, initially at least, failed to realize that whereas their own business was a 'high gloss' industry, building was a 'low gloss' industry. Computers cost more per cubic centimetre than most buildings cost per cubic metre. The building industry is the biggest in the country, but it is generally under-capitalized and few companies can afford to enjoy the relative safety of big capital holdings and still be competitive. Compared with its higher-gloss financial rivals, the aircraft and automobile industries, the building industry will expect computers on the cheap, and will be prepared to wait.

The developments in the small computer field have brought many new companies into computer production which should greatly improve the chances of the small specialist user getting the hardware he wants. The potential that these machines possess as an aid to draughting has been described in some detail in terms of the BASYS System. The significance of such a system, however, should not be seen solely in terms of drawing-office time and costs. The ability at any stage in the design to draw out automatically all the information so far collected, the capacity to delay the preparation of final working drawings to just before they are required, and the potential use of both standard details and product coding could have a significant effect on the architect's whole approach to design and office practice.

The ability to check rapidly all the information available on a design should add greatly to the efficiency with which this information is collected, and simplify the problems associated with drawing-office work schedules.

The capacity to delay the preparation of final working drawings until just before they are required will allow the maximum time for design and for assessment by the client before these drawings are prepared—which should minimize the risk of major alterations being introduced after they have been started.

Standard details within the office will not only aid in design and draughting, but will give the profession's chronic need for feedback on the performance of details a sense of reality. At present, when so many details are used only once, performance checks are often of academic interest.

The widespread use of these small computers in architects' offices should also serve to introduce the profession to computers and overcome the ignorance and fear which exists regarding them. The bureau terminal, in spite of certain limitations, is the most likely means by which the average architect's office will come to use a large computer, and the office system will provide a familiar and very convenient means for the user to input and output from the bureau machine.

The bureau terminal also provides the only practical way so far evolved for operating a product selection file. The object of such a file is, of course, to provide a rapid means by which the user can search the huge range of building products available for those most suited to a particular application. A small experimental file of this type is now in operation in London and the results so far are encouraging. The principal problem with such a file would appear to be the large costs of preparing and updating it, for this overhead is likely to exceed many times the computer running costs. No matter who ultimately organizes such a file, the cost will clearly have to be borne by the industry as a whole, that is to say by those who wish to sell the products as well as those who wish to find and use them.

Many computer applications at present being developed or under consideration may be relevant to the profession, and the possession of a terminal will, in some cases, be essential for their use. A national data bank of statistics, for example, is a possibility. Intended primarily as an aid to planning and sociological research, it could also prove of value to the profession.

When describing computers ten years ago, it was always necessary to distinguish between the digital computer and the analogue computer. The analogue computer, as its name implies, calculates using variable electronic pulses which are proportional to the values being used in the calculation. They depend upon a type of transformer which is able to manipulate these pulses with great accuracy. For general purposes the analogue computer went out of use about 1960, but may now stage a comeback as part of a new type of machine known as a Hybrid.

Certain forms of Hybrid computer have existed for many years in the field of machine tool control, but their use is now causing considerable interest in terms of general computation. The Hybrid computer consists of an analogue computer which is controlled by a small digital computer. The advantage of this combination is that for certain types of computation the analogue machine is very much faster than the corresponding size of digital computer, and this is particularly true where only approximate results are required and where the user wishes to discover the effect on the results of changing variables.

The digital computer's big advantage is that it can be programmed and does not need to be set up by hand, as the pure analogue machine has to be. This setting-up requires skill and usually a knowledge of the mathematics of the problem being solved. The digital computer, of course, requires neither, as this is all taken care of by the program. By combining a small digital machine with an analogue, the digital half can be programmed to control the analogue half. Work on Hybrid computers is at a very early stage, but as their potential is in the field of approximate solutions which is what the architect needs, and as, with a system like BASYS, the architect would already have a small digital computer, developments in this field should be worth watching.

Another possibly interesting development is that of specialist electronic calculators. These machines are small calculators containing a miniature core store, which has a series of pre-wired calculation procedures activated by a central panel of buttons and switches. Such machines can be 'programmed' by placing a perforated instruction card over the control panel and the calculation performed by following the instructions. The input and results are usually held in a numerical display, and values are inputted either from a keyboard or by some direct drawing measuring device. A leading example of this type of machine is the PLAN-CAL made by Romay AG of Zürich, Switzerland. This machine, which costs about £800 ($2000), is intended for the heating engineer and is marketed in England by Hoval Boilers Ltd. Heat loss and pipe run calculations are greatly facilitated by this machine and its set of programming cards, and the potential appears much wider. The operator using this particular machine guides a stylus

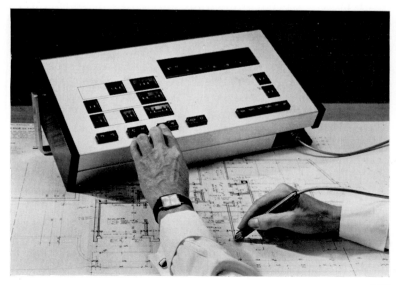

65
Hoval Calculator and measuring stylus

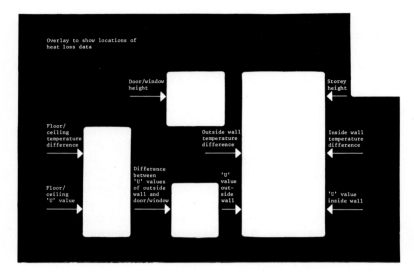

Overlay to show locations of
heat loss data

Door/window
height

Storey
height

Floor/
ceiling
temperature
difference

Outside wall
temperature
difference

Inside wall
temperature
difference

Floor/
ceiling
'U' value

Difference
between
'U' values
of outside
wall and
door/window

'U'
value
out-
side
wall

'U' value
inside wall

66
**Example of Hoval program over-
lay. This overlay shows procedure for heat loss calculations**

along any line on the drawing whose length he requires, having
first set the scale of the drawing on the machine. The present
stylus is accurate enough for heating calculations but is not
likely to provide sufficiently accurate values on small-scale
drawings to allow, for example, quantities to be measured. The
Swiss manufacturers are, however, about to produce a new
machine for general architectural use which will, it is claimed,
have a measuring device suitable for such applications.

7.2 Software Developments
The financial return to be expected in the near future from
marketing programs for architects is too unpredictable for the
subject to attract commercial exploitation and so the profession is largely dependent upon the universities to support work
in this field. Inevitably, research from this source tends to be
concerned with principles rather than with practice, and large-
scale strategic planning is a popular subject. Many projects are
in hand, however, which do fall within our present scope, but
in discussing them it is still necessary to distinguish between
the more theoretical researchers and those endeavouring to
prepare systems or programs for immediate use by designers.

The best-known work of the former type is that of a group led
by Nicholas Negroponte at the Massachusetts Institute of
Technology. The long-term aim of this group, who work over
a broad field and have an equally broad sense of humour, is to
replace the architect by an automaton. Their objective is to
improve design, not by aiding the designer, but by eliminating
both him and his human fallibility. Their work includes the
production of a simple map-reading robot, a study of the interaction between a computer-controlled machine and a family of
gerbils (i.e. small rat-like creatures) and a program, rather like

114

BAID-1, which assembles ten-foot cubes using a CRT display and light pen interaction. The plan to produce an architect-automaton is not to be taken too seriously, but this work could be of importance in helping to establish a theoretical basis for architect–computer interaction. Anyone interested in the work of this group should read Mr. Negroponte's book on the subject.[18]

Another piece of work which is worth noting, although to date it has had no practical application, is the program HIDECS-2 by Christopher Alexander and Marvin Mannheim.[19] HIDECS stands for the *Hierarchical decomposition of sets* and consists of a computer program which analyses the relationship between the numbers of a matrix by decomposing the matrix into a group of interrelated *sets* to the simplest form possible. This is demonstrated by an example in which thirty-three requirements are listed as being those which influence the shape of a group of dwellings in a city such as privacy, car parking, garbage collection, etc. The interrelationship of these thirty-three requirements is then decided and marked on a triangular matrix, rather like the association charts used for optimization (6.2) but without the use of rating values. The computer program then regroups the associations (1 to 33) into *sets* which display the minimum of interrelationship with each other. By this means the design problem is said to be clarified, as the designer can approach the final solution of the whole matrix by combining sub-solutions to each *set*. There have been a number of objections put forward to this technique including the basic objection that the relationships specified by the designer stem from his over-simplified preconceived notion of the system's operation (the system in this case being the group of dwellings). All the computer does is to spell out the system's operation in terms of *sets* from information provided by the designer who has laboriously converted the operations into relationships. The principal practical objection to the technique would appear to be the amount of time required to determine the relationships.

Several other programs have been prepared which are said to improve on HIDECS, but basically the objective is similar in each case.

In the field of design aids many groups and individuals are developing the approaches to basic architectural problems described briefly in Chapter 6. There are also a number of more technical problems under investigation, of which one of the most pressing is architectural aerodynamics.

Architectural aerodynamics is concerned less with the effect of wind forces upon buildings, as with the effect of buildings upon air movements in the spaces surrounding them. The violent gusting caused by high buildings often seriously detracts from the value of pedestrian areas around them, and although these effects have been studied, no theory exists by which they can be predicted. The aircraft industry's research has been concerned with air-supported bodies moving clear of the ground, which is a much more simple problem than the gust flow around a group of buildings resting upon it. Considerable success has been achieved, however, with wind tunnel experiments, in which gusting conditions have been reproduced by simulating not only the building being tested, but also the airstream conditions produced by existing or planned buildings down-stream of the area under consideration. Dr. T. V. Lawson of the University of Bristol, England, has gained considerable experience in this field, and although there appears little likelihood in the near future of a theory being devised to make these effects predictable, he is confident that reliable results could be obtained for new projects by interpolating those already obtained from many previous experiments. To interpolate such a complex pattern of results from many varied examples would require considerable computing power, but Dr. Lawson has suggested a technique whereby the designer could specify his proposed building shape and its surrounds and for a small cost assess the wind effects they are likely to produce. This is an example of the type of program which could be made available on a bureau terminal, to be used at the earliest possible design stage before ideas about overall shapes become hardened.

Several organizations have produced programs which are intended to be used at an even earlier stage of a project for the purpose of assessing the development potential of a site from an economic point of view. The Advanced Planning Research Group Inc. of Maryland, U.S.A., have developed a group of programs called 'The Housing Project Planning System'. These programs can be used to analyse the returns likely on a site using different types of development, and to prepare cash flowcharts for different building times, plus schedules of mortgage payments or rents. The value of such a program to the architect lies in the fact that it provides him with a painless method of investigating the financial implications of a wide range of development possibilities, so that he can assess the merits in this respect of solutions which may not have occurred to the client's other financial advisers.

7.3 Office and Education

The introduction of computer systems into architects' offices in the manner described would clearly bring about major changes in the method of working and in the composition of the typical office. The designer in charge of a project would be able to assemble personally the major sections and, except in the case of a very large project, he would also be able to prepare the final drawings and schedules unaided apart from the computer. Thus the project designer would be in a position to control and check the design much more closely than at present, while preparing most and possibly all of the information produced by the office.

Not only should this help to improve design quality but, by eliminating the four or even five echelons of staff down which information is passed within a large office, it should lead to considerable time-saving and greatly reduce the risk of error. The development of computer programs as an aid to architectural design is still at a very early stage, but in the more mathematically definable fields of the engineering sub-consultants the application of computers to take over the routines of calculation is already very advanced. Once the architect has mastered the use of the computer, there seems to be no reason why he should not apply these techniques to his own designs—if he were trained to do so. The training required, for example, in the comparatively limited field of building structures design should not take more than a year to master if a specific range of design and detailing techniques were taught for which suitable programs had been developed. A person so trained would, of course, not possess initially the experience required to design structures with safety, but only by practice is such experience gained.

The young university-trained engineer of today has little enthusiasm for the simple concrete or steel frames required by most buildings, and in the future it will become increasingly difficult to find men able and willing to design this type of structure. The architect will probably be offered either pre-fabricated standard structures or—when these cannot be used— standard details assembled by draughting staff to patterns specified by a design manual. The architect who has the overall design of the building in mind should, with suitable training, be able himself to do just as well with standard details and even better with a computer.

For the architect to realize the full potential offered by the computer, he will clearly require a new type of training which will provide a much more detailed knowledge of building design in its widest aspects. At present the schools of architecture are in an unhappy state. Soon after the Second World War, the majority gave up the Beaux-Arts system of teaching which had held sway for about a hundred years, and design became a matter of 'functionalism' with graph-paper façades and flowchart plans. As the concepts of function waned, the teacher of design found himself with little apart from his integrity to protect his own exposed idiosyncrasies. Left without the authority of a system, and in most cases unable to command sufficient personal respect to convince the student that mere good design is a valid objective, the present teachers of architecture have endeavoured to find new concepts by widening the field of study. Everything it seems is now relevant—from the social life of all to the mechanics of life in space—with little time or interest left for building. This is particularly true of some American colleges where the Johannes Itten type coloured paper projects of the traditional first-year class stretch on into the second and third years, to meet up with the regional planning of the fourth year and the world ecology survey of the fifth year, without ever, it appears, touching on building in between. This would be bad enough if present design standards were generally high, but as this is far from being the case, the situation is very serious. This is not to say that the type of training such schools give is not of value. We are rightly becoming more conscious of the methods we employ in attempting to plan our use of this earth, and there is a certain logic that such studies should have started in schools of architecture. What, however, is neither logical nor desirable is the fact that this development has in many places detracted from the study of building.

We now need to separate the two subjects and re-establish the teaching of architecture in terms of the total design of building. This is not going to be easy. Architecture, the art of building, is one which matures and which gives few prizes to youth. This is a consolation to most, but understandably is not a fact which attracts many students or potential students. The profession also has a social status which, in spite of their lack of enthusiasm for practising the art, is cherished by many who still wish to use the title.

This profession, like most others, must also accept that if its activities are to enter the realm of advanced technology, it will also become a subject requiring continuous study. If leisure is to increase in the future, the time necessary for each individual to maintain his own knowledge will become available. The profession, however, must provide facilities for the study required and this would best be integrated with normal professional practice at a local level, where every member would be able to contribute. If such a development is to provide maximum value to all, the information generated by this local effort should be cross-referenced and made widely available. Another obvious computer application.

7.4 Facts and Patterns

To predict the large-scale future use of computers by architects has required no crystal ball. The power of these machines is evident in many other spheres and their uses to the architect are clear. To foretell the impact that they will have on the profession, however, and to extrapolate from our present situation and prophesy their lasting influence, is not so simple. Just one unforeseen factor can upset so speculative a judgement and inevitably the author's own outlook must, to some degree, be biased.

118

Certain facts in our present situation, however, when considered together do suggest a pattern which, although tentative and possibly prejudiced, cannot be very far from that which should develop if the profession is to persist in its role of personal advisers and designers to the building client. The facts referred to are as follows:

1 If the architect is to retain the power to practise his art, he must re-establish his credibility as a technologist.

2 The architect's major technical problem is information handling and only the computer can solve this problem.

3 The application of office computer systems must greatly reduce the need for architectural assistance in the drawing office.

4 The profession has failed conspicuously to solve problems relating to certain building types. For example, the social problems which result from design decisions in mass housing are often not appreciated by the architect, and the attempts he makes to solve new problems are rarely explained to those who have to live with the resulting solutions. The future office will probably find it essential to have staff who will investigate new major projects and provide feedback after they are constructed by establishing contact with the users.

5 The teaching of architecture today is often diffuse and unrelated to the problems of building. The computer cannot provide a Beaux-Arts Nouveau System, but it can provide the means to total building design which is the only logical source from which the art of architecture could be revitalized.

6 It is possible that we are now dealing with the last generation of craftsmen on site. Also, the spread of higher education will almost certainly remove from the building site the large majority of those men who have always provided the necessary talent and experience required for on-site management. Prefabrication, with its need for increased accuracy of setting out and placing of components, will add to this problem and we may soon find it necessary to provide a similar level of site management to that required for civil engineering work today. If the architect's office was to supply this directly, a permanent on-site control could be established which would provide not only supervision of construction, but a day-to-day check on standards and finishes far beyond what is possible with the present system of weekly site visits. At present the management skills just do not exist within the profession to cater for this type of site organization. The engineers, however, have post-graduate management training courses for civil engineering contracts and there appears to be no reason why these facilities could not be provided for architects.

7 The advantages of having project managers from the architect's office are not limited to quality control. Of recent years many large projects have been seriously delayed by labour

disputes which have resulted largely from the loss of personal contact between operatives and management. When senior management is no longer seen to be actively engaged on a project, the operatives lose all sense of belonging to an organization and the allegiance previously engendered by the company easily falls prey to subversion. At the same time, as management becomes more concerned with the organization of a company and its taxes, the sites tend to be seen as malfunctioning critical path charts on the office wall.

If architects could provide site management with their greater consciousness of the social significance of a project and their contact with its ultimate users, they should be able to generate in the operatives a social awareness of the importance of their labour, which would help to improve the quality of building while at the same time creating a social pattern more in keeping with our times.

8 Many within the profession, who are deeply interested in the problems of building, will not feel that their capabilities are best applied in total design. Their skill in the sociological and management fields are essential elements in any future pattern of architecture. The young architect entering the profession will clearly need to gain experience in both the user study and site construction fields, and the balance between the need for designers and the numbers qualifying appears most likely to be met by the increasing need for these out-of-office activities.

7.5 Total Design

The architect has always looked for the majority of his commissions to the class which controlled the nation's wealth. The late eighteenth century and nineteenth century saw this wealth —which had previously been in a limited number of hands— spread to an enlarged middle class as a result of the development of commerce and industry. This century has seen the situation largely reversed, and the financial power of this country, and many others, is again concentrated in the hands of the State and a limited number of institutions. Each industry is now dominated by a few large companies whose individual inefficiency and low profitability has caused them to become financially unstable as soon as their growth is impeded. Social change and taxation have reduced the attraction of great personal wealth as its attainment no longer confers power, and to maintain it is practically a full-time occupation.

Thus only governments, who collect taxes, and institutions, who devote great skill to financial manipulation, are able in the long term to generate growth in their resources. Money is thus becoming institutionalized and is manipulated by specialists who provide loans and grants to individuals whom they judge best able to further the ends they deem desirable.

These individuals are numerous and varied: chairmen of

120

housing associations, heads of university departments, administrators of cultural centres, inventive engineers marketing new processes, all with an organization which ostensibly receives the money—but in practice it goes to back the enthusiasm and expertise of the individual.

An increasingly large part of the country's building programme is financed in this way, so these individuals are the new clients for whom the architect must design. Since their success at raising money has usually resulted from their enthusiasm and expertise, it is to be expected that they will look for these two characteristics to the same degree in their architects. This type of client exemplifies the need for the relationship which was discussed in the opening chapter, and so is best served by a small practice in which a single principal or a few partners are personally responsible for the design. Such a practice today, however, finds great difficulty in coping with all but very small projects. If a single job is undertaken which will involve the office fully for a year or more, then other work must be turned away; contracts are then lost and the future of the practice put in jeopardy.

The solution to this problem lies in finding the means to improve the productivity of an office by revolutionizing the information handling methods. The object of this book has been to describe computer systems which should provide such a solution, and by bringing their existence to the attention of the profession, stimulate discussion and a wider understanding of the computer's potential.

In order to make the maximum use of these developments, the architect must capitalize fully on both the computing capacity available and the programs provided for him by others. Each individual architect who acquires such a system will need to embark on a personal venture in this respect, building up his information and knowledge as time and the advent of new programs permit. Ultimately we should see emerge a profession proficient in these techniques and capable of what has been described previously in this book as total design. An architect who possesses such a capacity should feel confident as a technologist and would thus be freed mentally to concentrate on his responsibilities as an artist.

The future education of architects will obviously include training in the use of these systems, but the expansion of the present school syllabus to provide the theoretical background necessary for total design would require a major revision of the present teaching system. Such a change could, however, be gradual, beginning with a post-graduate year in total design and computer techniques, which, as the programs become available, could spread downwards into the final year. Later this spread could continue until the entire 'post-intermediate' years would be completely orientated to total design.

To envisage such a change, the administrators of a school of architecture would clearly need to regard the design of individual buildings as central to the architect's task.

The total design of a building, its planning and detailing both as a usable structure and as a thing of beauty, appears to some to be a tame, even irrelevant occupation when whole continents need to be planned and space explored. In fact the very reverse is true. The achievement possible within the confines of a single building site can be more valuable, both to the architect and society, than a lifetime spent on one of those more expansive projects, the vital significance of which so often becomes questionable long before it is completed.

To design a large building which serves its purpose well and does not offend those conscious of passing it on the street requires skill, sensitivity and hard work. To design one which gives real pleasure to many who see it and most who use it requires genius and the expenditure of great effort. To live to do this often is a capacity possessed by only a handful of men in every generation and they with justice are listed with the truly great of their age.

NOTES

LIST
OF
ILLUSTRATIONS

INDEX

NOTES

1. For further information about the Crystal Palace, see Patrick Beaver, *The Crystal Palace*, London 1970. Most of the original engravings first published in the *Illustrated London News* during 1850–1 are included in this book, apart from the very first illustration of the proposed building from which my top sketch was prepared. The introduction of the central crossing in the Hyde Park building was to allow a row of elm trees to be preserved. The profusion of vaults in the final design for Sydenham Hill represents, I think, Paxton's attempt to conform to contemporary canons of architectural composition as a result of reading the many critical comments made regarding the architecture of the earlier building.

2. A timber framed dwelling, of the type proposed by the *Timber Research and Development Association* for single house or apartment use, is the most practical form of construction to consider for this type of prefabrication. The finished weight of such dwellings would be of the order of 18,000 kg, leaving a margin of about 2000 kg for lifting tackle and wind shield. The most interesting machine proposed with this capacity is the Boeing HLH (heavy-lift helicopter) project which is being developed for the American armed forces. This machine will have a very sophisticated electronic system which will allow loads to be lifted and deposited very accurately under adverse weather conditions. It will, however, be a very expensive machine and this may cancel out its other advantages. The Russian MIL 10 is already in operation, but reports suggest that technical problems have arisen and so far, at the time of writing, only one has been exported. It has the required lifting capacity and when available should have a much lower initial cost than the Boeing. The Sikorsky Skycrane, in its present twin-engine form, has a lifting capacity of only about half the proposed requirement, but a three-engined version is reportedly being developed with a capacity nearer to my estimated requirement. It will probably be the cheapest of the three machines, the first to be readily available and, unlike the other two, a development of a machine with which experience has already been gained.

67
Boeing HLH

3. There are many textbooks from which one or other of these computer languages can be studied. For example Daniel D. McCracken, *A Guide to FORTRAN 4 Programming*, New York 1965 and *A Guide to ALGOL Programming* by the same author.

4. *The Penguin Computer Dictionary* is a very useful work that provides explanations for most of the terms the reader of this book is likely to require regarding conventional computers. The small computers discussed later in this book are best described in *Introduction to Programming. PDP-8 Handbook Series*, published by the Digital Equipment Corporation, and available through the company's local offices. Although this book describes a particular manufacturer's product, all small machines work in a roughly similar way. This is the best available description for the beginner, and has a useful Index–Glossary.

5. The CADMAC System has been developed by Dr. C. B. Besant and Mr. A. Jebb, with the assistance of Mr. R. E. Grindley, Mr. P. M. Saunders and Mr. A. J. Eagles. The project was sponsored by D-Mac Limited. The author conceived the BASYS programs and the package was prepared for operation using a PDP-8 by Mr. A. Hamlyn with the assistance of the CADMAC team.

6. Albert Farwell Bemis, *The Evolving House*, Volume 3, Cambridge, Mass., and London 1936. Bemis did not invent the idea of designing to a modular dimension, but he was probably the first to propose total coordination in three dimensions on a 4-inch modular grid. He adopted this particular module size, because the most common wall construction materials he saw used were 4-inch $\times$ 2-inch timber joists and 8-inch precast building blocks. The idea never gained favour in America where it was conceived. In Britain, however, in spite of the fact that the standard forms of wall construction involve $4\frac{1}{2}$-inch bricks to form 11-inch cavity walls, the 4-inch module has received considerable support and with the change to metric, the 100 mm module has become a recognized standard. The British building industry has a great need for a measure of dimensional control, so that the concept of modular standardization has great appeal. So powerful has it been, that for twenty years the advocates of total modular coordination have blinded themselves to the fact that it does not work. In practice it is only possible to coordinate dimensions of objects which lie in a single plane. The moment an object in another plane intersects the first plane, the object's thickness must be modular if it is not to upset the pattern. In practice, economy demands that building materials be used to the minimum practical thickness and this rarely corresponds to a module which is of practical value for the face dimensions of building components. For example, in Britain today, the official house planning module is 300 mm, but most partition panels have thicknesses of between 40 mm and 70 mm, so that at each intersection one panel must be a modular multiple, minus a thickness. This problem, and others, have defeated all attempts at modular coordination in housing and yet the concept is still widely canvassed and, as a result, little research has been undertaken to produce a more logical approach to dimensional standardization. Reading *The Evolving House* with hind sight, one can see the basic fallacies of modular coordination clearly outlined. Regrettably, Bemis died before his work was published. Had he lived to put his theories into practice, his remarkable book might have given him the influence to bring these problems to light twenty or thirty years ago.

7. For further details about this classification system, see the *CI/SfB Project Manual*, London 1970. The final chapter of this Manual (Part II, Section 3) is a brief explanation of CI/SfB, and anyone not already conversant with the subject will find the remainder of the book easier to follow if they first read this section.

8. *The NBA + BUILDING COMMODITY FILE* is an example of this type of product selection method. By publishing through the weekly journal

Building, the National Building Agency (London) is able to provide a regular updating of product information which is presented in tabular form. It appears that the Royal Institute of British Architects is planning a duplicate system as a by-product of its National Building Specification.

9. The BESS Program is being prepared in the Department of Engineering (Head of Department, Professor G. D. S. MacLellan), University of Leicester, under the supervision of Professor F. A. Leckie.

10. GENESYS was conceived and developed by Messrs. Alcock, Shearing and Partners, London, and has been implemented at the GENESYS Centre, University of Technology, Loughborough, Leicestershire. The sub-system Frame-Analysis/1 was also written by Messrs. Alcock, Shearing and Partners, and sub-system R.C. Building/1 by Messrs. W. V. Zinn & Associates, Sir Frederick Snow and Partners and Alan Marshall and Partners. Further information is available from the GENESYS Centre.

11. The emphasis in this chapter has been placed on the large programs that are concerned with the architect's own design processes. Many small programs have also been produced which assist in the solution of smaller building design problems such as heat-loss calculation, solar heat gain, shading of sunlight by obstructions, optimization of dwelling-room layouts and drainage design. There are also a number of specialist structural design programs available, such as the Space Frame Analysis Program available through the British Steel Corporation for use with their proprietary jointing system. The Environmental Advisory Service of Pilkington Brothers Limited, Liverpool, have a range of programs concerned with the design of glass-clad buildings, covering such subjects as heat gain, obstructional shading by other buildings and noise attenuation. A similar glass wall evaluation program is available through PPG Industries, Pittsburgh, Pennsylvania. These programs help to demonstrate the value of modern solar heat-reflecting glass by providing air-conditioning cooling load estimates for alternative types of glazing.

12. A detailed description of this technique is provided in an article. T. Willoughby, 'A generative approach to computer-aided planning: a theoretical proposal' *Computer Aided Design*, Autumn 1970. This article describes work carried out at the Institute for Land Use and Built Form, Cambridge, England.

13. The BAID Program was conceived and planned by the author with the assistance of Dr. Geoffrey Butlin and Dr. Roger Hubbald of the Computer Aided Design Workshop at the Department of Engineering, University of Leicester, England. Dr. Butlin and Dr. Hubbald also wrote the program.

14. Since this description was written, details have been published of a building appraisal program, PACE/1, which has been developed by Dr. T. W. Maver at the Architecture and Building Aids Research Unit, University of Strathclyde, Scotland. Details were published in *The Architects' Journal*, 28 July 1971.

15. The principal consultants for the Gyrotron Ride were Mr. Sean Kenny and Mr. George Djurkovic. The author designed the enclosing structures which were finally analysed using the computer program S.T.A.R., developed by Dr. Eric Solomon (Engineering Computations Limited, London). The main contractors were Douglas Bremner Limited of Montreal and the structures were supplied by ALCAN, the Aluminium Company of

Canada Limited. The joint used in the space frame was invented by Mr. Colin Grant and the testing of the joint/tube connection, as well as the investigation of the wind-excited oscillation problem, was carried out by Aluminium Laboratories Limited of Kingston, Ontario. Messrs. De Paoli and Borek were the Canadian associate engineers, and Mr. Jan Tomaka supervised the work carried out by ALCAN. For further details regarding the design of the space frame see Auger, Solomon and Alcock, *An Aluminium Space Frame Construction*, Paper J2, International Conference on Space Structures 1966, University of Surrey, England.

16. The stockbridge damper consists of two short cast-iron cups jointed by a stiff steel cable which is clamped at its centre to the object to be damped. The most common use for this type of damper is to stabilize high-voltage overhead power cables. For further details, see B. Auger, *Wind Induced Vibration in a Space Frame Structure*, Paper 23, Symposium on Wind Effects on Buildings and Structures, Loughborough University, England, 1968.

17. Parallax is defined in the *Concise Oxford Dictionary* as: Apparent displacement of an object due to actual change of point of observation. The architectural significance is that, to a moving observer, close objects pass his line of vision faster than more distant objects, thus providing rhythmical changes of pattern among groups of columns or other similar members such as the bars of a space frame. Architecturally this effect has been consciously applied throughout history from the hyperstyle halls of ancient Egypt to the Miesian glass and steel offices of the twentieth century.

18. N. Negroponte, *The Architectural Machine*, Cambridge, Massachusetts, and London 1970.

19. Alexander and Mannheim, *HIDECS-2: A Computer Program for the hierarchical decomposition of a set, with an associated linear graph*, Civil Engineering Systems Laboratory Publication No. 160, Cambridge, Massachusetts. The HIDECS method of sorting is now slightly out-of-date, and many more sophisticated techniques have since been developed. However, Alexander was the first to apply such a technique to architectural problems and, so far, no work appears to have been published which describes any similar applications. A general review of the theoretical work in this field is provided by Lance and Williams, 'A General Theory of Classificatory Sorting Strategies', *Computer Journal*, Volume 9, page 373.

68
Stockbridge damper

LIST OF ILLUSTRATIONS

The illustrations used at the head of each chapter are from *Le Diverse et Artificiose Machine* by Agostino Ramelli, 1588. This book describes and illustrates nearly two hundred machines for assisting in, among other things, both the construction and destruction of buildings. It was brought to my attention by Mr. D. E. Dean, the Librarian of the Royal Institute of British Architects, from whose copy the blocks for this book were made.

Except when otherwise stated all the drawings are by the author and were lettered by Gillian March.

INDEX